A Bicentennial Malthusian Essay

Thomas Robert Malthus
(1766-1834)

"The power of population is indefinitely greater than the power in the earth to produce subsistence for man." 1798

A BICENTENNIAL MALTHUSIAN ESSAY

Conservation, Population and the Indifference to Limits

JOHN F. ROHE

Rhodes & Easton
TRAVERSE CITY, MICHIGAN

Published by RHODES & EASTON
121 E. Front Street, 4ᵗʰ Floor, Traverse City, Michigan 49684

Publisher's Cataloging-in-Publication Data
Rohe, John F.
  A bicentennial malthusian essay: conservation, population and the indifference to limits / by John F. Rohe — Traverse City, MI : Rhodes & Easton, 1997.
     p.   cm.
  Includes bibliographical references and index.
  ISBN 1-890394-00-9
  1. Malthus, T.R. (Thomas Robert), 1766-1834. 2. Population. 3. Malthusianism. 4. Human ecology. I. Title. II. Essay on the indifference to limits.

HB863 .R64   1997
304.6—dc21   97-66724

Frontispiece: THOMAS ROBERT MALTHUS *(copyright © British Museum)*
Jacket photograph courtesy Gary Williams: NYMPHAEA ODORATA
Text design by Donna L. Theriault

PROJECT COORDINATION BY JENKINS GROUP, INC.

00 99 98 ✠ 5 4 3 2 1

Printed in the United States of America

*To Karl, and his schoolmates
in the Class of 2002,
that our legacy becomes
their undiminished future.*

CONTENTS

PREFACE

The Earth belongs in use to the living . . . no man can by natural right oblige the land he occupies, or the persons who succeed him in that occupation, to the payment of debts contracted by him. For if he could, he might during his own life, eat up the use of the lands for several generations to come . . . then the Earth would belong to the dead, and not the living . . . No generation can contract debts greater than may be paid during the course of its own existence.
— Excerpt of a letter from Thomas Jefferson to James Madison.

THIS ESSAY WAS written to illuminate a root cause of threats confronting our successors. It focuses on a disease. Not a symptom. While the effects of harm are "out there," a root cause is to be found "in here." In our hearts, our minds, our passions, hopes and aspirations, many of which are well-intentioned. Here lies a root cause. It was first examined by Thomas Robert Malthus in 1798. His message retains relevance today.

We express concerns over global warming, ozone depletion, contaminated groundwater, toxic waste, degraded habitats, endangered species and lost biodiversity. We readily identify each of these as a threat to the legacy we may someday leave. By relying on principles set forth in the Malthusian *Essay* of 1798, this *Bicentennial Malthusian Essay* identifies these threats as mere symptoms of a more serious disease: our indifference to limits. The indifference can result from a lack of interest, shortage of insight, educational deficiency, blind faith, unwillingness to consider alternatives or a variety of other causes. Whatever the origin, this indifference bears a fearsome quality.

9

We live in a world of limits. Historic illusions of a flat earth extending into infinity have now been replaced by space shuttle snapshots of an illuminated gem cloaked by a resilient ecosystem.

A select few species will tend to predominate in an ecosystem.[1] In our case, the species, homo sapiens, has developed a sense of self-consciousness and the technological means to modify its surroundings. Vis-a-vis other forms of life, this species has a hefty appetite, it tends to eat high on the food chain and leaves a formidable trail of troublesome waste in the wake of its progress.

Mankind's biorythyms keep pace with nature's cadence, but the progress of our environmental degradation follows the beat of a different drummer. Accordingly, the trail of harm can become imperceptible from our vantage. So we not only degrade the surroundings, but we lack the means to responsibly assess the loss.

Perhaps this is because our biological timepieces do not resonate with delayed consequences. Maybe we're adept at maneuvering in the short-term, but lack the ability to react to long-term changes. We do not readily perceive ongoing environmental decline.

The romantic mystique of the frontier has captured the imagination of Americans for centuries. Pioneer fur traders penetrating our deep forests saw an inexhaustible supply of beaver pelts. Legendary loggers, such as Paul Bunyan, envisioned an inexhaustible white pine harvest. Inexhaustible mineral lodes gave rise to thriving mining communities. The illusions of unending resources resulted in vanishing beaver populations, a productive white pine harvest spanning only a few decades and abandoned ghost towns where mining communities once prospered. Even the sky blackening migration of the passenger pigeon have now been diminished to a few statuesque museum relics and a cherished folklore.

We know this is a finite planet. We just don't know exactly how many people spaceship earth can accommodate. But there are limits. We also don't know how many wetlands can be destroyed before water becomes unfit for human consumption. But we know there are limits. We don't know just how much the solid waste stream can be increased before a landfill moves in next door. But we know there are limits. And

---

[1] Edward O. Wilson, *The Diversity of Life*, Harvard University Press, 1992, Pg.164.

we still don't know how many carbon dioxide molecules the atmosphere can safely accept. But there are limits.

1998 marks the bicentennial of *An Essay on the Principle of Population* by Thomas Robert Malthus. In this classic and controversial work, Reverend Malthus ponders prospects for the human experiment. Will human numbers eventually outstrip the carrying capacity of a land mass?[2]

Malthus recognized human populations have the power of excess reproduction. In other words, fertility can increase the number of people beyond the land's ability to sustain them. Crossing the perilous carrying capacity threshold came to be known as the "Malthusian crunch." Fertilizers, irrigation, genetically engineered hybrids and technology have enabled mankind to push back the limits (the "Malthusian shuffle"). But can technology provide solutions for unlimited growth on a finite planet?

Population numbers build on growing base numbers. A 1.5% increase of 100 people is nominal. But 1.5% of 6 billion humans at the Malthusian Bicentennial is not nominal. Over time, the multiplication of a growing base produces an overwhelming surge.

A geometric quality in population numbers was readily apparent to Malthus. Eventually, the growing number of people will consume available resources (the "Malthusian trap"). We may successfully expand the carrying capacity of a land mass in the short term. But can we stake our children's future on the perpetual expansion of carrying capacity to accommodate unlimited growth in human numbers, consumption and waste products?

Two hundred years ago Malthus confronted a prevailing lack of awareness. His essay was a reactionary document. Although he never used the specific words, his essay awakened the citizenry to their "indifference to limits." And today, the conservationist is still reacting to a similar mind set. The indifference to limits has solidly burdened our basic assumptions and convictions. Shedding this load is no easy

---

[2] Carrying capacity has been defined by the Carrying Capacity Network as the number of individuals who can be supported without degrading the physical, ecological, cultural and social environment, i.e. without reducing the ability of the environment to sustain the desired quality of life over the long term. The Carrying Capacity Network (CCN) is a nonprofit organization in Washington D.C.

undertaking.

At the bicentennial of the Malthusian essay, our indifference to limits is no longer limited to human numbers. Were Thomas Robert Malthus writing today, he would likely find our indifference exists on a broad terrain. We are insensitive to fossil fuel limits, atmospheric pollution limits, economic growth limits, urban sprawl limits and consumptive limits, to name a few. In this bicentennial essay, indifference is categorized in three basic divisions: human population growth, economic growth and growth on the land.

The face of our indifference peers back at us from degraded habitats, endless highways, polluted rivers, urbanized lakes, burgeoning landfills, vanishing forests, lost wetlands, forgotten population issues and from the abandoned people in abandoned urban centers. This indifference remains as much a root cause of our destructive potential at this Malthusian bicentennial as it was 200 years ago, when education was available only to the elite few. In view of current educational standards, the present indifference may even take on a more sinister quality. Today, it may be an act of aggressive indifference, active suppression or determined denial of evolving food shortages, global warming, ozone depletion, interpersonal conflicts from crowding, urban sprawl and degraded surroundings.

ACKNOWLEDGMENTS

THERE ALWAYS SEEMS to be more to learn from his questions than from his answers. He was employed in the business community, yet he had an abiding apprehension over the prevalent affinity for growth in the financial world. My father often pondered whether we would ever consider negative growth as a positive development. This question was heretical at the time, and it still is today. Yesterdays' heretic can become tomorrow's prophet. First and foremost my father deserves recognition in these Acknowledgments.

It is a privilege to know Mary Lou Tanton and John H. Tanton, M.D. Most of us are humbled by their tireless and generous efforts in population issues. In her other life, Mary Lou donates time to a low vision clinic. Her husband, John, as an ophthalmologist, brings the world into focus for others. They have shared the gift of sight in their professional spheres. Their primary contributions, however, are in sharing the gift of foresight.

Some of the following persons may be bemused by their recognition in the Acknowledgments. Discussions with, and assistance from, these valued friends and colleagues have influenced the ideas expressed in this book. By remembering them here, they should not share in the shortcomings in this work, as accountability for its failings remains exclusively with the author. Thank you Wil Cwikiel, Gail Gruenwald, Robert Kyser, Wayne Lutton, Gustav A. Uhlich, M.D., Gary Williams, Justin Rashid, Jim Olson, Frederick M. Baker, Jr., Ellen J. Preisman, Richard C. Preisman, M.D., William B. Conn, Keith Schneider, J. K.,

13

Karen Cole, Julie Stoneman, S.M., Rick Neumann, John Mack, Joel Moore, Tim Flynn, David Payne, Paul Rondell, Mary Whitmore, Doug Dow, the New England Aquarium in Boston, Massachusetts, the Petoskey Public Library and many others. Thank you, Rhodes & Easton, and particularly members of its publication staff, Jerrold Jenkins, Alex Moore and Mark Dressler.

I remain particularly grateful for the good fortune and privilege of working with my co-worker, Donna L. Theriault, and for the companionship of my wife, Debbie, over the past two decades.

Part One

THOMAS ROBERT MALTHUS

1

CHILDHOOD AND OPTIMISM

IT WAS 10 years before the American Revolution would be fought and 10 years before the steam engine would be invented. On February 13, 1766 he was born the sixth of seven children in Surrey, England, and he reached adulthood at about the time of the French Revolution. His name, Thomas Robert Malthus, eventually became an adjective. "Malthusian" is now synonymous with population concerns.

At the time of his childhood, England was a pre-industrial, agrarian society controlled by landed aristocrats. Education was reserved for the few, and not at all for women. Class distinctions were rigid. Medical treatments were practiced, but often involved a greater risk than the apparent illness.

Industrialization gradually improved the comforts of life for some (and it no doubt made life worse for others, as evidenced by the writings of Charles Dickens). Matters we now take for granted must have imparted profound changes to the daily lives of persons at the time. Even our eventual placement of a colony on Mars is not likely to affect our daily lives nearly as much as the initial industrial advances did theirs. Travelers moved from horseback to a motorized form of transport. Weather patterns no longer affected travel plans as before mechanized transportation. These initial advances were accompanied by a burgeoning sense of optimism for mankind.

This is the setting in which one of history's most controversial thinkers emerged.

He answered to his middle name, Robert, not Thomas. In 1791, he was ordained a priest in the Church of England and became known as Parson Malthus. As a professor of history and political economy in the

East India College at Hertfordshire, he was affectionately known as "Pop" by his students.

A congenital cleft palate left him with a speech impediment, although in his later years he is said to have had a pleasing voice. He married at age 38 and fathered three children, two of whom survived to adulthood. And that's where the family tree ended. Neither of his surviving children bore children of their own.

2

REACTIONARY

THE OPENING SENTENCE of the Malthusian essay suggests it was written as a reaction. Robert was reacting to the conventional optimistic wisdom of the time. The opening sentence states:

> The following Essay owes its origin to a conversation with a friend, on the subject of Mr. Godwin's Essay on Avarice and Profusion, in his Enquirer.

William Godwin, the optimist, had an abiding belief in the perfectability of man. In his essay *Of Avarice and Profusion*, written in 1797 (one year before the Malthusian essay), Godwin states:

> There is no wealth in the world except this, the labour of man . . . Wealth consists in this only, the commodities raised and fostered by human labour.

The corollary to "no wealth" without "human labour" is that an abundance of wealth follows from an abundance of human labor. More humans translated into more wealth.

In 1752, David Hume also wrote of the advantage of large populations:

> But if everything else be equal, it seems natural to expect, that wherever there are most happiness and virtue and the wisest institutions, there will also be most people.

The more the merrier was a fashionable sentiment at the time.

Robert's father, Daniel Malthus, was a friend of Jean Jacques Rousseau, David Hume and William Godwin. Daniel shared their optimistic belief in the progress of mankind which, in time, was expected to reach a state of "perfection."

Robert questioned the belief in mankind's progress. Would progress lead to a state of perfection? Or would it lead elsewhere?

Although he did not use these terms, he brought the notion of "excess reproduction" to the forefront. He noticed a geometric progression to human numbers over time: 2, 4, 8, 16, 32, 64, 128, 256, etc. He also believed food production would, in time, fall tragically short for the demands of geometrically growing human populations.

While living at home, and while serving as an ordained priest in the Church of England, Robert had frequent discussions with Daniel, his father. Robert resisted his father's optimistic belief in mankind's path toward perfection because the primary requirement of subsistence; namely, food, would eventually be outstripped by human numbers. That is the "Principle" of his essay. Daniel may have disagreed with his son's principle, but he was sufficiently intrigued to encourage his son to write about it. Robert complied with his father's wishes and wrote an essay on this principle.

While his contemporaries believed increasing human numbers were a decisive blessing, Robert would suggest there may be an inverse relationship between the quality and the quantity of human life. A German translator defined Malthus' maxim: "There should be no more people in a country than could enjoy daily a glass of wine and a piece of beef with dinner."[3]

Robert made two basic observations:

> First, That food is necessary to the existence of man:
> Secondly, That the passion between the sexes is necessary, and will remain in its present state.

He then concluded:

---

[3] Patricia James, *Population Malthus*, Routledge & Kegan Paul, London, 1979, p. 363.

> Assuming, then, my postulata as granted, I say that the power of population is indefinitely greater than the power in the earth to produce subsistence for man.

So then what? What happens when we overshoot the earth's subsistence powers? When human numbers exceed the carrying capacity of a land mass? Robert responded to the optimist's hope for perfectability. He envisioned misery and vice where they saw perfectability.

Today, we may draw an analogy between the Malthusian principle and a thermostat. The thermostat controls room temperature. Warmth turns the furnace off when a critical temperature is reached. Falling temperatures turn it on. Similarly, when human population reaches a critically high level, it will be brought in check by another control. Malthus identified the mechanism of control as misery and vice. When population dwindles, the prospect for excess reproduction eventually increases human numbers to the critical level. This allows for another bout with misery, vice and the "Malthusian crunch."

When excess reproduction in human numbers confronts the limit, misery and vice could be expected to bring human numbers within the land's carrying capacity. The terms "misery and vice" were carefully chosen. Misery refers to population control by non-human intervention and vice references human intervention. Misery can be thought of as starvation, famine, disease, and pestilence. Vice, on the other hand, involves active human participation. War and infanticide are examples of Malthusian vice.

This 1798 essay, in the face of prevailing optimism, became a well-read and highly controversial text. It was initially published anonymously.

MALTHUS AND DARWIN

O NE OF THE essay's most influential effects would not come to fruition for another 40 years after it was published and four years after Malthus died. This essay prompted a thought process which would challenge the intellectual underpinnings of every self-conscious society. It would forever change the way we see ourselves and our relationship to the surroundings.

The day after reading the Malthusian essay, another Englishman stumbled across the logical effect of excess reproduction. He was keenly interested in fossils and natural history. The following is from Charles Darwin's autobiography:

> In October, 1838, that is, fifteen months after I had begun my systematic enquiry, I happened to read for amusement Malthus on *Population,* and being well-prepared to appreciate the struggle for existence which everywhere goes on from long-continued observation of the habits of the animals and plants, it at once struck me that under these circumstances favourable variations would tend to be preserved and unfavourable ones to be destroyed. The result of this would be the formation of new species. Here, then, I had at last got a theory by which to work.[4]

Were it not for the Malthusian essay, would the theory of evolution

---

[4] Nora Barlow, *The Autobiography of Charles Darwin,* (1876; reprint, London, Collins, 1958) p.120.

and natural selection have remained secretly entombed in the fossil record? Would we still arrogantly see ourselves as residing far above nature? Would we still lack the humility to envision ourselves entwined as a fragile thread in nature's web of life?

Malthus has, in some circles, retained his image as the cheerless killjoy of the late 18th century. But he will forever claim a monumental bookmark on history's pages for unlocking Darwin's imagination. Notions of evolution and natural selection would challenge virtually all prevailing biblical, social and cultural beliefs. And Darwin knew they would. Accordingly, he did not publish the account of natural selection for another 21 years after Malthus sparked his thoughts. Darwin's *Origin of Species* was published in 1859, and only at the time another Malthusian inspired writer, Alfred Russel Wallace, was about to reveal his independent discovery of natural selection.[5]

---

[5] Daniel C. Dennett, *Darwin's Dangerous Idea*, Simon & Schuster, 1995, p. 66. Peter Vorsimmer, "Darwin, Malthus and the Theory of Natural Selection," *Journal of the History of Ideas*, 20 (1969), 527-46.

THORNS AND ROSES

GODWIN AND HIS utopian peers saw nothing but roses for the human prospect. Malthus, on the other hand, was also a believer in mankind, but he appreciated how we can have too much of a good thing. He perceived an indifference to limits in the euphoric optimism surrounding pre-industrial England in the late 18th century. Although he did not know exactly where the limits might reside, he was sensitive to their existence.

Though he was controversial, and though he tended to spoil the utopian party, he nevertheless remained steadfastly committed to his "ultimate object": "to diminish vice and misery." Hardly an uncharitable perspective.

His concern for others, his amiable character and his good-natured manner endowed him with rich friendships. Even David Ricardo, his tenacious foe on economic issues, had enduring respect for Malthus: "I should not like you more than I do," Ricardo wrote, "if you agreed in opinion with me."

Malthus may have sensed a certain inevitability to the prospects for starvation. Did this make him cold-hearted? Or was he wildly compassionate? Today, almost one billion people go to bed hungry every night.[6] Many slip beyond the brink of malnutrition every day. This weighed heavily on him before the present drama materialized.

Even though he thoughtfully contemplated the long term human prospect, he was often not seen in a benevolent light. Shelley, the poet, and son-in-law of William Godwin, characterized Malthus as "a eunuch

---

[6] Lester R. Brown and Hal Kane, *Full House*, W.W. Norton & Co., 1994, p. 37.

and a tyrant" and also as "the apostle of the rich."[7] Charles Dickens derided Malthus with his fictional Ebenezer Scrooge, who quipped that the poor might be dispensable and "decrease the surplus population."[8]

Was Malthus a passionless, cold-hearted, calculating and miserable miser? Was he the "squeezing, grasping, covetous old sinner" inspiring Dickens' fictional Scrooge? Or, was he the likeable, compassionate chap hoping to avert disaster before it befell civilization? Was he behind the times? Or, was he out front? Did he spoil the party for some? Or, did he try to keep it going for others? Was his recognition of limits warranted? Or, do we live in a boundless world of plenty?

---

[7] F. L. Jones, Ed., The Letters of Percy Bysse Shelley, (2 Volumes); Oxford, 1964.

[8] Charles Dickens, A Christmas Carol, London, 1843.

Part Two

POPULATION GROWTH

UP A CREEK

These facts prove the superior power of population to the means of subsistence in nations of hunters, and this power always shows itself the moment it is left to act with freedom.

It remains to inquire whether this power can be checked and its effects kept equal to the means of subsistence, without vice or misery.
—Malthus, 1798, Chapter III

THE LAST GLIMPSE of summer's abundance is now overshadowed by the heavier hue of darkening clouds. A crisp chill in the wind overhead blurs the distinction between summer's quickened pace and autumn's deceleration.

The sun and earth inch away from fall's equinox as they proceed toward a seasonal appointment with winter's solstice. The forest becomes aflame with scarlet and crimson playing in the light and shadows of the broken canopy's expanding holes. As leaves depart from summer's manufacturing sites, the autumn sun floods the ground. A soft carpet of red, orange and yellow dapple the forest floor. Summer's yielding twigs become brittle and snap sharply.

An unruffled calm accompanies this change of season, yet the forested world still glistens with life. A disquieting peace masks nature's restless pulsations. Insects still creep ponderously along decaying snags as oppressive summer heat gently yields to autumn's crisp chill.

In the restless silence, one of nature's great seasonal migrations unfolds. The salmon,[9] impelled by the season, keeps its primeval date at the headwaters.

Now in its fasting mode, the female salmon tenaciously strains against the river's current. She crowds the edge for a peaceful respite. She fights the murmuring waterfalls. She navigates the bends and forks on a timeless path. The early salmon may have started this seasonal ritual in North America during the Middle Eocene Epoch about 50 million years ago.[10]

Scaling 12 foot waterfalls is not beyond her reach. Even in these final days, and while fasting, her aging body thrusts against the advancing stream. While straining to hurdle a froth-filled waterfall, her tail continues to wag on the airborne ascent. When striking the rushing waters, she's still furiously stroking. Once underway, she doesn't skip a beat. Her fins continue to unleash a thrust of force by recoiling on the foam.

She might, with luck, break the waterfall on the first try, but there's a good chance she won't. If she's swept back by the tumbling waters, refuge will be sought behind a rock or in a calm bend. After regaining strength, she's ready to strike again. She'll be more deliberate in her approach this time. Resolve will be mustered at the base of the falls.

When ready to again proceed, no stroking opportunity will be lost in the ascent. The price of momentary hesitation is another speedy and disheartening plunge to the base of the falls. She'll build momentum in the swirling chaos and bolt from the crest of a standing wave[11] as though momentarily weightless. With good fortune, she'll strike the smooth reflective crest of the waterfall. A final burst of energy slips her beyond the ridge and she then safely continues on her enduring date with creation. The time and place of this date were prearranged by her predecessors, and she passionately struggles to comply.

She's been programmed to conquer the waterfalls and to follow

---

[9] Salmonidae, Oncorhychus.

[10] Karl Albert Frickhinger, *Fossil Atlas Fishes*, 1995, p. 617.

[11] Jerry Dennis and Glenn Wolff, *The Bird in the Waterfall*, Harper Collins Publishers, 1996, p. 122.

designated forks in the stream. Her migratory instincts are remarkably consistent with those of her ancestors. Guided by familiar scents, she navigates the same path as has her mother and her mother's mother over the ages in this ageless ceremony.

As she continues on her upstream migration, the forest contour changes. The soft lowlands blend into a mature upland hardwood forest. This is where her life began and it will also mark her final resting place in this endless cycle. Here the dense canopy resists the changing season. Slanted beams of light are filtered by the canopy's autumn hue. Light does not drench this forest's floor. Rather, beams are selected. The select streak through. These softened rays gently probe the ferns, the mosses, and the clear, rapidly flowing stream where the female salmon searches for a bed of gravel.

During summer's torrential storms, newly exposed glacial debris tumbled into this ever-changing stream.[12] She attentively inspects the valued deposits strewn along the river bottom next to other ice age stones and rocks deposited in prior years.

In the raging silence of this deep forest, she clings to the last vestige of life while fulfilling her final mission.

The female red salmon's[13] prior silvery color becomes a bright red hue during mating season. The male develops a hooked snout, green head and a red body to match his mate for the festive occasion. In a modest courtship dance, she deposits her eggs on a bed of glacially ground remnants under the attentive gaze of her male suitor. He sweeps in to fertilize the eggs and she follows close behind to stir the stream bottom. Glacial pebbles and stones are swept by her fins to provide a protective cover for life's latest treasure.

The male and female, having left a promise of life on the stream bed, are now content to surrender their weakened bodies to nature's unbroken sequence. While the world of associations still throbs with color, their mental connections vanish. In the unsettling emptiness of autumn's austerity, their decaying remains provide nourishment to

---

[12] Daniel B. Botkin, *Our Natural History*, G. P. Putnams's Sons, 1995.

[13] Salmonidae, Oncorhychus, Nerka.

myriad life forms around them. The vulture lingering on the wind patiently waits for carrion to wash ashore.

The scene bristles with improbabilities. Of the 7,500 eggs laid by the female salmon on a bed of gravel, only 4,500 will hatch. The hatched eggs are called "alevin." The alevin measure approximately 15 mm when newly hatched. They furtively remain in the gravel deriving nutrition from a yolk sac until this food source is depleted.

By the time summer's brightly flowered meadows bring fresh vitality, when mother nature's invisible hand brings a lush abundance to the scene of endless rhythm and beauty, just when seasonal signs of life abound, the 4,500 alevin are substantially reduced in number. Of the 4,500 alevin, only 650 survive to become tiny free swimming fish. At this stage of their development, they are known as "fry" or informally "small fry."

There's no lasting sorrow for the high mortality of newly-hatched alevin leashed to their life-giving yolk sac. For the death of any creation in nature, there's a corresponding life. The nourishing yolk sacs empower others in this rich ecosystem as salmon molecules spiral up the food chain in a new season of life.

The 650 "fry" find themselves relatively defenseless to prevailing risks in these sparkling waters. Eventually, the fry develop dark transverse markings on their sides. They then become known as "parr" or "brandling." Of the 650 fry, only 200 will outlive this phase to become "parr" or "brandling."

The 200 parr meet the risks of river life for approximately two years. They then develop a silvery color and become known as "smolt." Of the 200 parr, only 5 smolt survive as nature's endless cycle endures.

The five silvery smolt will then descend to the sea, backtracking the course of their parents' upstream migration several years ago.

One of the five smolt will succumb to the chill stare of a predator while at sea. The four other adult salmon will survive a few years by munching their way through small fish and crustaceans.

Eventually they will return to the river of their birth. It will then be their turn to undertake the ancestral upstream migration to primeval breeding grounds. In their waning days, the four adult salmon will begin a terminal fast and again challenge the surging waters in this final test of strength. Only the most vibrant will endure the challenge with sufficient strength to complete the solemn mating ritual in the headwaters.

The 7,500 eggs have been reduced in number to a mere four returning adults. Of these four survivors, only two will repeat the mating ritual in which 7,500 eggs are once again swept beneath a layer of gravel after fertilization.[14]

We might be troubled by the cruel reality of nature's harsh hand of fate dealt to the salmon. Of the 7,500 eggs, only two adults survive the grim statistics of life to repeat the ancestral mating ritual. This harsh reality is tempered by recognizing the salmon are temporary sojourners in nature's timeless wonder. The endless cycle of life. The rich mosaic. The intricate threads from which even we emerged.

Market specimens of sockeye salmon[15] generally weigh 10 to 20 pounds. Another species, the Chinook Salmon[16] can often grow to more than five feet in length and weigh over 100 pounds.

In a less hostile environment, perhaps four adults, rather than two, could mate. This means the odds that one of the 7,500 eggs will eventually mate would have increased from 2/7,500ths to 4/7,500ths. This rather insignificant change in the salmon's survivability sweepstakes translates into a monumental change for the planet. Instead of the two mating salmon replicating only themselves at the end of the next generation's struggle, there would now be four. Their number would therefore double in a single generation.

The two mating salmon, weighing ten pounds each (totaling 20 pounds) will now become four mating salmon, ten pounds each (40 pounds). The next generation will find 80 pounds of mating salmon. One hundred sixty pounds will appear the next year, then 320 pounds, 640 pounds, 1280 pounds, etc. At this pace, it won't take long to reach

---

[14] The mortality rate for salmon was courteously provided by the New England Aquarium of Boston, Massachusetts, where these statistics accompany a thought provoking display.

[15] Salmonidae, Onchorynchus, Nerka.

[16] Salmonidae, Onchorynchus, Tshawytscha.

awesome numbers. After only 50 generations, the cumulative weight of the salmon's descendants will be 22,500,000,000,000,000,000 pounds.

Fossilized remains of salmon suggest they have inhabited North America for approximately 50 million years. If the salmon population continued to double every generation during this 50 million year period, the universe, as we know it, would consist of nothing but salmon.

The sea hare decorates seaweed with millions of tiny defenseless eggs in ribbon-like structures. An American Oyster sheds 500 million eggs per year. The North American Meadow Vole can give birth to 9 offspring per litter and 17 litters per season. Each newborn can become fertile within a few weeks following its birth. Two mating voles could, in a single season, leave millions of descendants. At the other end of nature's fertility spectrum, the female Orangutan has a single birth every six years. But the world isn't overpopulated with sea hare, oysters or voles. Nor have orangutans become extinct (yet). The defenselessness of offspring in sea hare, oysters and voles requires them to leave more offspring. Intensive maternal care and improved prospects for survival of the infant Orangutan lead to reduced fertility, yet a balance is maintained.

The statistical odds of a salmon egg maturing to adulthood and surviving to mate are only 2 in 7,500. But if it were any higher, the salmon would carry the seeds of their own eventual destruction (the universe would not comfortably accommodate this level of reproduction). And if the reproductive prospects were any worse, say 1 in 7,500, then their numbers would drop by one-half every generation. Under these odds, 128 returning salmon would become 64 the next generation, then 32, then 16, 8, 4, 2 and eventually only one salmon would struggle up a creek for its homecoming. Who would rescue this salmon from its sexual predicament?

The sparkling waters and murmuring waterfalls camouflage nature's finely tuned wager. Darwinian forces are more adept at anticipating surging numbers than we seem to be.

6

SURGING NUMBERS

That population, when unchecked, goes on doubling itself every twenty-five years, or increases in a geometrical ratio.
—Malthus, 1798, Chapter II

Y OU'LL WANT TO use a thin sheet of paper for this experiment. Say there are 72 sheets to the inch. Now fold the single sheet once. Fold it a second time. And if it is big enough, fold it 40 times. How thick would the resulting stack of folded paper become? A few inches? Maybe a few feet? Perhaps as tall as you are?

The answer is that there isn't a sheet of paper big enough for the experiment. The resulting folded paper would span from the Earth to the moon![17] It is over 241,000 miles in thickness.

Notice the thickness doubles with every fold. In other words, this is an "exponential" progression. We started with one sheet, one fold created two sheets of thickness. The next fold created four, then eight, then sixteen, thirty-two, sixty-four, until we reach the average distance

---

[17] Here's the math. With every fold, the paper doubles in thickness. A single fold produces two sheets of thickness. That's two to the first power. Two folds is two to the second power; four sheets. Three folds is two to the third power; eight sheets. Forty folds is two to the fortieth power; that's 1.099511 times ten to the twelfth power. That's how many sheets of thickness there are in forty folds. The rest of the equation simply equates this into miles. The number of sheets must be divided by the following formula: 72 sheets per inch multiplied by twelve inches per foot, multiplied by 5,280 feet per mile. The result is 241,019 miles. This is slightly above the average distance from the Earth to the moon.

from the Earth to the moon.[18] It only takes forty doublings to get there.

If the experiment continues, you'll soon want to convert to fireproof paper because the scorching sun is only nine more doublings away. A few more doublings will find you folding paper at the edge of the solar system. Best to leave this for the professionals. Don't try it at home.

Edward O. Wilson, of Harvard University, points to a similar exponential progression by using the example of a lily pond:

At first there is only one lily pad in the pond, but the next day it doubles, and thereafter, each of its descendants doubles. The pond completely fills with lily pads in 30 days. When is the pond exactly half-full? Answer: On the twenty-ninth day.[19]

Just one more daily doubling fills the pond. From the vantage of a single lily pad, there might be little reason for concern on the twenty-ninth day. One half of the pond is still open. There would still appear to be ample room for an abundance of growth, but it's an illusion. On day 29, the lily pads will engulf the pond in a brief 24 hours.

Imagine a test tube filled with nutrients. A single bacteria dropped into the nutritious mix will thrive. It will multiply and divide in every generation. For some bacteria, a generation consists of only 20 minutes.[20] The descendants of this single bacteria will prosper until shortly after one-half of the test tube nutrients are depleted. At the halfway point the bacteria, if they could see, would still firmly believe

---

[18] Donella H. Meadows, Dennis L. Meadows and Jorgen Randers, *Beyond the Limits*, Chelsea Green Publishing Co., 1992.

[19] Edward O. Wilson, "Is Humanity Suicidal?," *The New York Times Magazine*, May 30, 1993, pp. 24-29.

[20] Garrett Hardin, *Living Within Limits*, Oxford University Press, 1993, p. 88. Dr. Hardin also points out that fruit flies have a population doubling time of 50 hours. Humans, according to the unintended experiment on the Bikini Islands, had a population doubling time of 13 years. Elephants, by Darwinian fate, have a doubling time of 35 years.

in vast resources and unlimited frontiers. But in reality, the descendants of the original bacteria are now only a single generation (20 minutes) away from encountering a common and abrupt fate. In just one more doubling of bacterial life, the bacteria will fill the tube. The seemingly abundant nutrients of 20 minutes ago will be fully depleted.

Meadows, Meadows and Randers invoke a Persian legend in making the same point:

> The surprising consequences of exponential growth have fascinated people for centuries. There is an old Persian legend about a clever courtier who presented a beautiful chessboard to his king and requested that the king give him in exchange 1 grain of rice for the first square on the board, 2 grains for the second square, 4 grains for the third, and so forth.
>
> The king readily agreed, and ordered rice to be brought from his stores. The fourth square on the chessboard required 8 grains, the tenth took 512 grains, the fifteenth requires 16,384, and the twenty-first square gave the courtier more than a million grains of rice. By the fortieth square, a million million rice grains had to be piled up. The payment never could have continued to the sixty-fourth square, it would have taken more rice than there was in the whole world.[21]

The authors also invite their readers to personally experience the effect of exponential growth: "Try eating one peanut on the first day of the month, two peanuts on the second day of the month, four peanuts on the third, and so on. Try to guess in advance on what day you'll have to give up this exercise!"[22]

A *one million year* oil supply would be depleted in 928 years if annual consumption increased by only 1.5% per year. (1.5% is a rough

---

[21] Donella H. Meadows, Dennis L. Meadows, Jorgen Randers, *Beyond the Limits,* Chelsea Green Publishing Company, 1992, p. 18.

[22] Id, Chapter 2, fn. 3 at p. 255.

approximation of the annual human population increase.) Numbers surge under exponential pressures.[23]

Population numbers also have a tendency to surge.

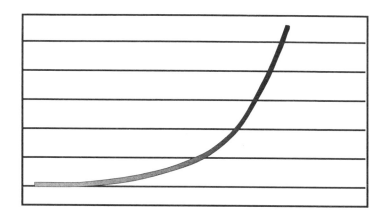

FIGURE 1. EXPONENTIAL GROWTH

Globally our numbers double in approximately 46 years.[24] How many more doublings will spaceship Earth accommodate? At the Malthusian bicentennial there are about six billion of us. Can we ethically allow this experiment to run its unaltered course?

From the vantage of a lily pad, it was deceptively simple to conclude the pond was still widely receptive to growth on the 29th day. Similarly, our "wide open spaces" are an illusion in the face of the exponentially surging quantity of human protoplasm. There are almost one billion people now bordering on starvation.[25] They would freely testify to the

---

[23] Lindsey Grant, *Juggernaut*, Seven Locks Press, 1996, example using 2% at p. 8.

[24] Lester R. Brown and Hal Kane, *Full House*, W.W. Norton & Co., 1994, p. 58.

[25] Lester R. Brown and Hal Kane, *Full House*, W.W. Norton & Co., 1994, p. 37.

harsh reality of food shortage (i.e., people longage[26]). Many of them receive only one meal per day. They go to bed hungry. And many slip beyond the brink of malnutrition every day. Any variation in the price or supply of food will bear hardest on their grim mortality statistics. In Malthusian terms, misery and vice beckon.

In the 1950s, total births exceeded total deaths every year by about 50 million. In the 1960s, net annual world population gains were 60 million. In the 1970s, we added 70 million every year. The 1980s added about 80 million annually. The third millennium could see us adding 100 million additional people every year. That's total annual births minus total annual deaths!

Present fertility rates eventually reach the absurd. If population growth rates continue, in a few hundred years every woman, man and child will have one square meter of ice-free land on which to work, live, play, grow their food and bury their dead.[27] Twenty doublings of the population will leave a mere .7 millionth acre of arable land for each person.[28] Stephen Jay Gould sarcastically carries the absurdity still one step further:

> . . . in a few centuries, for example, humans will form a solid mass equal to the volume of the earth and no escape into outer space will be possible because the rate of increase will cause the diameter of this human sphere to grow at a speed greater than the speed of light, which, as Einstein taught us, sets an upper bound upon rapidity of motion.[29]

Naturally, we'll never reach these wildly absurd scenarios. Just how

---

[26] Garrett Hardin, *Living Within Limits*, Oxford University Press, 1993, pp. 309 and 310.

[27] Lindsey Grant, *Juggernaut*, Seven Locks Press, 1996, p. 8.

[28] Paul R. Ehrlich and Anne H. Ehrlich, *Betrayal of Science and Reason*, Island Press, 1996, p. 211.

[29] Stephen J. Gould, *Full House*, Harmony Books, 1996, p. 96.

will the human experiment play itself out when we bump up against limits between the real now and the absurd then?

Absent an abrupt confrontation with Malthusian misery and vice, a decline in human numbers will not occur until long after we acknowledge population as a concern. After World War II, Japan recognized an imbalance between people and available resources. It provided extensive family planning, free contraception and encouraged couples to have no more than two children. The effort was exceptionally successful. In 1945 the annual Japanese birth rate was 34

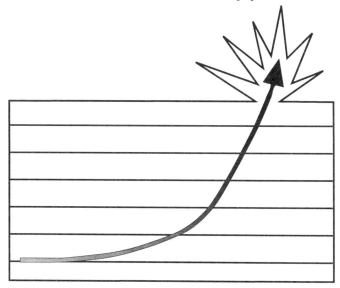

FIGURE 2. EXPONENTIAL GROWTH CONTINUED

births per 1,000 people. A brief 15 years later, by 1960, it dwindled to 17 per 1,000. One would expect the Japanese population to plummet as a result of this abrupt drop in fertility. But it did not. In fact, during the same 15 year period the Japanese population increased by 20%. It went from 75 million in 1945 to 90 million in 1960! How could population continue to soar while fertility was cut in half? Demographers tell us it has something to do with momentum. It is like applying the brakes to your car. The car does not immediately stop at the first sight of a danger in the road.

Similarly, when the global community recognizes a problem with population and decides it is time to respond, human numbers will not precipitously drop (absent a monumental calamity). Younger members must first move through their fertile years before reduced fertility is reflected in total numbers. That's why Japan's population continued to grow between 1945 and 1960.

In order to decide whether it is now time to be concerned about our numbers we must ascertain where we will be in another generation or two. Where we are today is of little relevance. A reaction time must be considered. This is akin to the reaction time in applying the brakes to a motor vehicle. At 20 mph, a motorist will travel 22 feet before their foot moves from the accelerator to the brake. This results from the average reaction time of 3/4 second. At 30 mph, the motorist will travel 33 feet during the reaction time. At 80 mph, the motorist will travel 88 feet.[30] As the net population increase continues to surge, year after year, our "reaction time," like the reaction time for the motorist at higher speeds, carries a more formidable threat.

---

[30] Data derived from Affiliated Adjusters, Inc. Information Tables at website: http://idaho-web.com/aai/tables.htm.

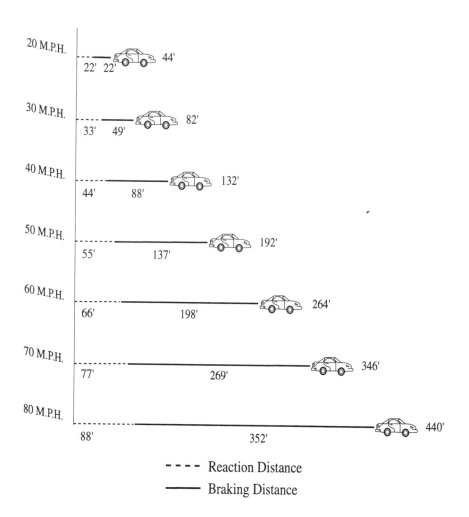

FIGURE 3. REACTION AND BRAKING DISTANCE.

The reaction time only allows time for the motorist to move their foot from the accelerator to the brake. Once the brake pedal is depressed, the "braking distance" can be computed. As the vehicle moves faster, a greater distance is required. At 20 mph the braking distance (as distinguished from the reaction time) is only 22 feet. At 30 mph, it is 49 feet. At 40 mph, it is 88 feet. And at 80 mph the braking distance is 352 feet.[31] As human numbers continue to spiral upward, reaction times and braking distances loom as a greater hazard.

Our response to population concerns, like braking distances, are subject to a number of variables. The tire type, car weight, pavement type, pavement temperature, moisture and snow or ice conditions will influence braking distances. Similarly, variables such as politics, education, church, social conditions, and competitive breeding among races or religions will affect the reaction time and braking distances for population.

Population increases are also analogous to the velocity of a freight train heading downhill toward a cliff. Both build momentum as they grow. The issue is whether we can summon a sense of foresight before the cliff comes into plain view and it is too late to apply the brakes.

Though our population discussion may be punctuated by coughs induced by airborne irritants and toxins, we'll blissfully dismiss population concerns based on a well-known biblical mandate. A divine decree. We can't possibly be a menace to ourselves because it has been said on high that we "be fruitful and multiply."[32]

Lame excuse. It didn't say: "be fruitful and overpopulate beyond the brink of extinction when it's too late to slam on the brakes." Rather, it is a biblical mandate to "be fruitful and multiply." And if we can't multiply . . . if we don't understand how exponential numbers multiply and surge, then we've been handed a divine decree to go back to school.

---

[31] Data derived from Affiliated Adjusters, Inc. Information Tables at website: http://idaho-web.com/aai/tables.htm.

[32] Genesis 1:28.

7

DOUBLING TIMES

*In the United States of America, where the means of subsistence
have been more ample, the manners of the people more pure, and
consequently the checks to early marriages fewer, than in any of the
modern states of Europe, the population has been found to double
itself in twenty-five years.*
— Malthus, 1798, Chapter II

ONE MIGHT CONCLUDE the lily pad or the bacteria were indifferent
to limits. They were also unaware of the driving force behind doubling
numbers. The seeds of indifference sow a fateful crop.

We, on the other hand, may be the first species with the knowledge
and self-consciousness to foresee limits and to recognize the prospect
of extinction. We have a simple, albeit slightly inexact, tool in
measuring doubling times. It involves the number 70.[33]

Would you like to compute how long it takes for your money in the
bank to double if it collects interest at the rate of 5% per annum (and
you ignore tax implications)? Simply divide 70 by the interest rate of
5%. 70 divided by 5 is 14. In other words, your money will double in
about 14 years.

At 7% per year, your money will double in 10 years. (70 divided by
7 equals 10.) At 10% interest, your money will double in 7 years.

In a slow growth year, our economy might plod along at a lackluster
growth rate of a mere three percent. At this rate, the economy will
double in 23 years (70 divided by 3 = 23.33). This means there will be

---

[33] Bartlett, Albert, A., "Forgotten Fundamentals of the Energy Crisis," *The Journal of
American Physics*, 1978, reprinted by the Environmental Fund, Monograph Series.

four doublings in the lifetime of a 92 year old person. At that time, the economy would therefore be 16 times as large (four doublings is: 2, 4, 8, 16). If the present level of economic activity poses a threat to our natural heritage, imagine the risk resulting from sixteen times this activity level.

If a three percent growth rate is a matter of concern, consider the bill of goods promoted by our politicians. During the 1996 presidential campaign, vice presidential candidate Jack Kemp professed he would like to see our GNP grow at the rate of 5% per year. That's a doubling time of 14 years. (70 divided by 5.) In a healthy lifetime of 98 years, that's seven doublings! The progression of seven doublings is: 2, 4, 8, 16, 32, 64, 128. Does he really think the annual GNP can be 128 times as big in a single year sometime later in the lifetime of a child born today? In 98 years? That's 128 times as many new homes in a single year, 128 times as many new roads in a single year, 128 times as many new cars, planes, boats, skyscrapers and televisions all in a single year. 128 times the present activity level in less than a century! He's either indifferent to limits, or he has secreted his utopian escape hatch from the rest of us.

In light of seemingly insurmountable environmental challenges resulting from existing activities, imagine cranking up the heat 128 times. If a political candidate ran on a platform of increasing our activity 128 fold, we would be on our guard. But when it is couched in terms of pro-growth rhetoric, it becomes seductively appealing.

An affinity for growth reduces to an absurdity. Let's assume we maintain a steady growth rate of 6% per year. This is close to the U.S. rate of growth in the early 1980s and less than the present rate in some Asian countries. If we can maintain this rate of growth, the economy will be 339 times as big in a period of 100 years. It is even more daunting to think that in just an additional 50 years we will be reproducing 100% of all items having economic value today in a single 24 hour period! In other words, every road, house, car, television and other item of existing value today will then be manufactured in a single day![34] Anyone want to be around for that?

The economic community is awkwardly dividing itself into "pro-growthers" and "no-growthers." Defining the debate by "growth" is deceptive. The debate is about sustainability. There are sustainability advocates, and others who can't be bothered to think about notions of sustainability. Let's be truthful with our labels.

Sustainability advocates are woefully outnumbered. Check the business section of any news report. The prevailing assumption is growth is good and more growth is better. You're not likely to find any musings on just how much of a good thing is good for us.

Is there a conspiracy? Or are we just not programmed to think exponentially? Maybe we lack the hard-wiring. Maybe prophetic genes were not selected for in the fossil record. Could they have suffered a Darwinian fate eons ago?

---

[34] For the mathematics afficionado, this is computed by determining when 1/365th of the annual growth equals the first base number. In other words, if we assume the total economy has a value of 1 today then, at a given rate of interest, how long will it take for the economic growth in a single year to total 365? Owners of the Hewlitt-Packard HP12C can program this calculator to perform this computation as follows: First clear the program register with: f, PRGM. Then: P/R, i, 1, CHS, PV, 0, PMT, 36500, ENTER, RCL, i, ÷, FV, n, P/R. In order to run the program, select your rate of interest and press R/S.

8

EXTINCT PROPHETS

If I saw a glass of wine repeatedly presented to a man, and he took no notice of it, I should be apt to think that he was blind or uncivil. A juster philosophy might teach me either to think that my eyes deceived me, and that the offer was not really what I conceived it to be.
— Malthus, 1798, Chapter I

FORTY-PERCENT OF AMERICANS breathe air unsafe by federal standards.[35] One thousand U.S. communities fail to meet clean water standards.[36] Approximately 15 million Americans now drink from unsafe water supplies.[37] Lakes and streams are off-limits to swimmers. We are cautioned to limit our consumption of fish from the Great Lakes, which comprise 20 percent of the world's fresh surface water. We relentlessly elbow into natural havens and nudge the biodiverse heritage aside. Our national parks are loved to death.

Grim signs of environmental degradation abound. Yet we vigorously oppose environmental laws standing in the way of the fast buck. We'll hoist a banner of property rights. We'll use the word "wise" in excusing a clear-cut. We'll profess ozone depletion is a hoax. By biblical mandate, chauvinism or divine intervention, we'll believe population concerns are heretical. Yet, paradoxically, we will also cherish our

---

[35] Associated Press, "Air in 43 Urban Areas Fails to Meet Federal Standards," October 21, 1994, *Washington Post.*

[36] Roy Beck, *Re-Charting America's Future,* The Social Contract Press, 1994, p. 20.

[37] Zero Population Growth, In Troubled Waters, Summer, 1990 Fact Sheet.

children and earnestly hope to leave them the blessings of a lasting legacy.

How can the paradox be explained? Are we so mesmerized by the lure of short-term economic gain that long-term well-being is obscured? Is it inconceivable that a single species could inflict lasting harm upon a planet? Has our conquest of natural systems been too recent to leave an enduring mark on our conscience?

Or, might our short-sightedness be more organic in nature? Three prolific writers in this field seem to think so. First, curator of entomology at the Museum of Comparative Zoology, Harvard University, Edward O. Wilson:

> The brain evolved into its present form during this long stretch of evolutionary time (the last 2 million years), during which humans existed in small, preliterate hunter-gatherer bands. Life was precarious and short. A premium was placed on close attention to the near future and early reproduction, and little else. Disasters of a magnitude that occurred only once every few centuries were forgotten or transmuted into myth. So today the human mind still works comfortably backward and forward for only a few years, spanning a period not to exceed one or two generations. Those in the past whose genes inclined them to short-term thinking lived longer and had more children than those who did not. Prophets never enjoyed a Darwinian edge.[38]

Biologists Paul and Anne H. Ehrlich have written extensively on population, conservation biology, co-evolution and environmental ethics. They share Edward O. Wilson's view:

> A major part of the problem, of course, is that all of us have difficulty perceiving large-scale or slowly developing environmental problems. Human beings evolved, both

---

[38] Edward O. Wilson, "Is Humanity Suicidal?," *The New York Times Magazine*, May 30, 1993, pp. 24-29, and *In Search of Nature*, Island Press, 1996, pp. 186 and 187.

culturally and genetically, in situations in which there was no advantage to perceiving changes occurring slowly, decade by decade. People have been programmed to react quickly and appropriately to sudden environmental change, as when a leopard appeared in the path ahead. But there was no advantage to registering a change in climate— if it occurred, it was not human caused, and there was precious little a band of hunter-gatherers could do about it except seek greener pastures. Indeed, there is reason to believe that our nervous systems evolved to keep the general environmental backdrop of our lives seemingly constant in order to allow us to concentrate on short-term changes happening against that backdrop.[39]

Lindsay Grant, a prolific writer on population and public policy, also finds our indifference to population issues results from Darwinian selection:

Humankind is fast descending into times of trouble, and the troubles are largely of our own making. The human tribe, or parts of it, has faced disasters before, but this is not a natural disaster. We can stop the Juggernaut if we recognize the sources of our problems and mobilize our fractured energies.

Unlike the Indian Juggernaut, population growth is invisible to most people. The numbers are visible enough. Try a visit to Calcutta or New York. But the growth is almost imperceptible. We try to adjust to its gradual effects rather than confront it. History is a slow-moving panorama, and each human peers at it through the narrow lens of one lifetime. As a species, we do not handle long-term problems very well. Our early ancestors survived by their ability to escape a predator or catch a fast-moving prey, not by

[39] Paul R. Ehrlich and Anne H. Ehrlich, *Betrayal of Science and Reason*, Island Press, 1996, pp. 42 and 43.

contemplating environmental change. It is the human propensity to accommodate to population change rather than address it that makes this particular Juggernaut so dangerous.[40]

The ability to perceive future harm of present actions does not come easy. An indifference to limits was prevalent at Malthusian times and it remains so today. It is pervasive and it does not discriminate. No one is exempt. It affects the perceptions of the meek as well as the prominent. For example, in 1992, the U.S. Supreme Court decided a property owner might be entitled to governmental compensation because he was denied a permit to build on a fragile and frequently submerged dune. In ruling against the government, U.S. Supreme Court Justice Scalia approvingly quoted from E. Coke in 1812:

For what is the land but the profits thereof?[41]

Is this now the land ethic of the highest court in the land? Will our children excuse us from looting the land and frittering away their future so long as we're motivated by the "profits thereof"?

A similar indifference to limits was betrayed by Aubrey Wagner, Chairman of the Tennessee Valley Authority in the 1950s. TVA was, at the time, becoming the world's largest purchaser of strip-mined coal. The Chairman stated:

Strip mining, while it is going on, looks like the devil, but if you look at what these mountains were doing before the stripping, they were just growing trees that were not even being harvested.[42]

The Darwinian selection process may have made it difficult for us to

---

[40] Lindsey Grant, *Juggernaut*, Seven Locks Press, 1996, p.3.

[41] *Lucas v South Carolina Coastal Council*, 505 U.S. 1003 (1992).

[42] Otis L. Graham, Jr., *A Limited Bounty*, McGraw-Hill, 1996, p. 50.

consider the big picture, the bird's eye view, the long road ahead. But it also left us with a compelling affinity for our tribe, our successors, our kin, our children. We inherited a strong sense of reciprocal altruism for members of our group, how ever the group may be defined.[43] Will our acquired sense of compassion and foresight overcome the prehistoric indifference to limits? Will altruism to our successors empower us to perceive long-term changes?

Our forebears wanted to improve the lot in life for their followers. Encyclopedias are brimming with information on individual contributors. Each generation of improvement was layered upon the one before. This culminated in our present level of comfort. We're now living off the cumulative historic, inter-generational goodwill. It is packaged in the cloak of what we call civilization. Will we carry this generous progression into the future?

---

[43] Robert Wright, *The Moral Animal,* Vintage Books, 1994; Natalie Angier, *The Beauty of the Beastly,* Houghton Mifflin Company, 1995; Frans de Waal, *Good Natured,* Harvard University Press, 1996.

9

CARRYING CAPACITY

Must it not be acknowledged by an attentive examiner of the histories of mankind, that in every age and in every state in which man has existed, or does now exist,

That the increase of population is necessarily limited by the means of subsistence.

That population does invariably increase when the means of subsistence increase. And,

That the superior power of population is repressed, and the actual population kept equal to the means of subsistence, by misery and vice.
— Malthus, 1798, Chapter VII

W E CO-PLANETEERS HAVE imparted monumental alterations to our speck of cosmic dust. The lasting imprint occurred during civilization's momentary blip on history's time screen. Projecting the prior effects of human activity into the future prompts questions relating to "carrying capacity."

The phrase "carrying capacity" imparts a thought process on sustainability. Just what level of activity is sustainable? How many people? How much economic growth? How large the waste stream? These questions involve a fundamental choice. Either we decide to think about limits, sustainability and the carrying capacity of land mass, or we decide not to be bothered. Not to decide is to decide. The absence of thought, a default position, is the functional equivalent of deciding not to be bothered.

The reality of our earthly predicament is that we remain embedded in the surrounding ecosystem. The rich mosaic of life and the biodiverse fabric not only becomes the fount of our imagination, but it is also essential to the survivability of the human species.

Notions of carrying capacity relate to the integrity of this web of life upon which we rely. A sustainable web provides a secure safety net. Unsustainable activities assure our successors will no longer be cradled by a rich mosaic of life and perhaps not be cradled at all.

Each species in the web carves its historic niche in an ecosystem. Symbiotic relationships exist among all forms of life in nature's endless cycle of energy exchange. There are redundancies in the system. Accordingly, some extinction and abuse can be tolerated. Some threads in life's biodiverse web can, in fact, be destroyed without pauperizing the system. But there's a limit.[44]

Paul Ehrlich draws an analogy to rivets in an aircraft. Some can safely be popped in mid-air, but eventually a critical point is reached. The removal of just one more rivet will then cause the system to crash. We impoverish the system at our peril. Pushing nature's limits ultimately tests the carrying capacity.

There are two primary components in determining the carrying capacity of a land mass: the assimilative capacity and the productive capacity.

The assimilative capacity refers to the environment's ability to absorb waste. The Great Lakes, for example, can absorb more pollutants, sewage, chemical runoff and storm sewer discharge than the babbling brook in your local park. The environment has an ability to break down and recycle many chemicals in its never-ending energy flows. The limited absorptive capacity cannot be exceeded without degrading the lives of our successors.

The productive capacity, on the other hand, considers the sustainable yield of the land. A land mass can only produce a limited quantity of food or life. A portion of the plant and animal life is needed to

---

[44] Reed F. Noss and Allen Y. Cooperrider, *Saving Nature's Legacy*, Island Press, 1994; Chris Maser, *Sustainable Forestry*, St. Lucie Press, 1994; William S. Alverson, Walter Kuhlmann, Donald L. Waller, *Wild Forests*, Island Press, 1994.

regenerate itself in the next season. Some is needed to maintain interdependencies in a biodiverse mosaic of life. A portion is also available for human consumption. The second prong of carrying capacity relates to this productive capacity of the land.

Garrett Hardin's image of a "commons" in his classic essay "The Tragedy of the Commons"[45] initially referred to the productive capacity of land (how many head of cattle could be supported by the land mass over the long term). Yet his image has become a metaphor for the absorptive capacity of the environment. Dr. Hardin describes the Tragedy of the Commons as follows:

> The tragedy of the commons develops in this way. Picture a pasture open to all. It is to be expected that each herdsman will try to keep as many cattle as possible on the commons. Such an arrangement may work reasonably satisfactorily for centuries because tribal wars, poaching, and disease keep the numbers of both man and beast well below the carrying capacity of the land. Finally, however, comes the day of reckoning. That is, the day when the long-desired goal of social stability becomes a reality. At this point, the inherent logic of the commons remorselessly generates tragedy.

Suppose the herdsman adds one head of cattle to graze on the commons. The herdsman would derive 100% of the profits from his one additional head. But notice the additional burden on the land is imposed on the community at large (the commons). So the single herdsman derives all the benefit from one additional head, but the burden is distributed among all others. In Hardin's parlance, the costs have been "commonized." Dr. Hardin explains how each herdsman's logical thought process leads to tragedy:

> Adding together the component particular utilities, the rational herdsman concludes that the only sensible course for him to pursue is to add another animal to his herd. And

---

[45] Garrett Hardin, *Science*, Vol. 162, p. 1243-1248, 13 Dec 1968.

another; and another . . . But this is the conclusion reached by every rational herdsman sharing the commons. Therein is the tragedy. Each man is locked into a system that compels him to increase his herd without limit— in a world that is limited. Ruin is the destination toward which all men rush, each pursuing his own best interest in a society that believes in freedom of the commons. Freedom in a commons brings ruin to all.

Today, Dr. Hardin's metaphor of the "commons" retains its relevance. Instead of imposing upon pasture land held in common, we encroach upon other properties held in common. For example, smokestack emissions and groundwater contaminants intrude upon the absorptive capacity of air and water owned in common with everyone. The polluter singularly retains the profits from the polluting activity while sharing the toxic burdens freely with all users of air and water. Air, water and other environmental "sinks" have become the modern day "commons." The "Tragedy of the Commons" is as relevant today as it was several centuries ago.

Ours isn't the only species confronted with the prospect of excess reproduction. Natural forces cause species to make regular concessions to the carrying capacity of their ecosystem. The lemming is a small rodent. If they overpopulate the ecosystem, stress disease sets in and their numbers will dwindle.[46] All forms of plant and animal life capable of excess reproduction rub up against the carrying capacity of their environment. Millions of seeds are dispersed, yet only an insignificant fraction locate a safe bed of nutrients, sunlight and water. The rest exceed the carrying capacity and suffer the dire consequences.

The population numbers of many species oscillate with existing conditions, as they are held in check by the carrying capacity. The lynx and the rabbit, for example, are directly related to each other in the food chain. Rabbits provide the primary source of nutrition for lynx. As the prodigious rabbit population increases, more nourishment becomes available to the lynx and correspondingly more lynx will

---

[46] Desmond Morris, *The Human Animal,* Random House, 1994, p. 115.

survive. The greater number of lynx present a greater threat to the rabbits. Accordingly, as lynx population increases, the rabbit population begins its decline. As rabbits are eliminated, the ecosystem provides less nourishment for the lynx. In other words, the carrying capacity of the land for the lynx will decline with fewer rabbits available. The lynx population will plummet soon after the dwindling rabbit population. As there are fewer lynx, there will be fewer threats to the rabbit. Accordingly, the prolific rabbit population will again surge. And the number of lynx will follow as nature's endless oscillation continues to hover around the land's carrying capacity. The cycle is known as "overshoot and oscillation."[47] When this carrying capacity is exceeded, the system does not crash. It oscillates.

If human populations overshoot the carrying capacity of planet earth and leave a degraded, polluted, irradiated and impoverished ecosystem, will we bounce back like the lynx? Or is it more likely that the system will be too hostile for human life? Will we "overshoot and oscillate" or is it our destiny to "overshoot and collapse"?

Technological advances have boosted the carrying capacity for humans. Yet, surging populations cannot stretch the carrying capacity indefinitely. Our ancestors would take pride in the legacy left for us. But how would they view our propensity to carry the tradition forward? Our inability or unwillingness to consider the future (a species of indifference to limits) hinders the effort. Perceptions may, however, be aided by collapsing the history of the earth into a more human time frame. We may then see ourselves as a mere fleeting moment in finite space on the trajectory of time.

---

[47] Donella H. Meadows, Dennis L. Meadows, Jorgen Randers, *Beyond the Limits*, Chelsea Green Publishing Co., 1992, p. 123.

10

A FLEETING MOMENT

So diversified are the natural objects around us, so many instances of mighty power daily offer themselves to our view, that we may fairly presume that there are many forms and operations of nature which we have not yet observed or which, perhaps, we are not capable of observing with our present confined inlets of knowledge.
— Malthus, 1798, Chapter XII

HISTORY ENABLES US to define ourselves against a colorful backdrop. It illuminates the past and foreshadows the future. By locating our place on the trajectory of time we capture a glimpse of where we are and where we may be headed. And if we don't know where that might be, then any road will get us there. Marcus Tillius Cicero, (106-43 B.C.), stated:

History is the witness that testifies to the passing of time; it illuminates reality, vitalizes memory, provides guidance in daily life and brings us tidings of antiquity.[48]

In contrast, Henry Ford reminds us that "history is more or less bunk."

Our sense of history may be limited to the "oldies" on a radio station, or in some cases, American history. Even the study of early civilizations will take us back a few thousand years, at most. That's history, as we know it.

But we haven't even scratched history's surface. By exploring molecular structures, scientists have determined the once molten rock, which we know as planet Earth, is currently celebrating its 4.5 billionth

---

[48] Marcus Tullius Cicero, *De Oratore*, II, 36.

birthday. In other words, the Earth is now 4,500 million years old. This history, when viewed from the perspective of time frames around us, renders the 5,000 year history of human civilization a mere blip on the screen.

Assume a 24 hour clock represents the entire history of planet Earth.

At midnight, following a Big Bang, the newly formed molten rock begins to coalesce with other fragments to develop the Earth's gravitational field. The first form of microscopic life[49] begins to form at approximately 3:30 a.m. At 8:00 a.m., slimes and molds move from salt waters to claim a foothold on rocks around the edges of tidal pools.

Then, at about 10:30 a.m., the first cells with a nucleus,[50] ancestors of our own cells, make their debut.

The Earth's atmosphere was predominantly CO_2 until life's process of photosynthesis captured it and released oxygen to the air. It was not until shortly after noon that atmospheric oxygen reached a critical level. Then, other forms of life could use this reactive gas to burn carbon for energy-consumptive activities. Geologic processes sequestered the carbon as hydrocarbons such as coal, oil and natural gas.

Until approximately 8:00 p.m., life was confined to primitive forms, such as bacteria. But then, distinctive plant and animal forms of life began to appear in the seas. These early forms of life left the first skeletal fossil record for their inquisitive successors.

Between 8:00 p.m. and 9:00 p.m. marine life exploded in diversity. During this brief one hour interval, sex was invented. Sensual life forms could now experiment with their sexuality. The mix-em-up frolics in this newly discovered sexual revolution gave rise to a rapid mixing of genetic material. Combinations were selected, others were discarded, and there was a burst of biodiversity. New forms of life flourished and became increasingly competitive in the ecosystem.

By 9:00 p.m. the first hard-shelled fossils left their mark in our prehistoric quarries. At 9:45 p.m. the first animals would be seen creeping among the primitive forests. At 9:52 p.m. the earliest woody

---

[49] Prokaryotes.

[50] Eukaryotes.

plants appeared. A rigid structure enabled trees to become formidable competitors in a new vertical race for a place to bask in the sun.

Shortly before 11:00 p.m. amphibians began losing ground to reptiles and the age of the dinosaurs was underway. By 21 minutes before midnight, the era of the dinosaurs abruptly ended. Scientists theorize the sky blackening debris from a massive asteroid collision rendered the cold-blooded dinosaurs extinct. Warm-blooded mammals then acquired a competitive edge. This event closed a colorful chapter in the fossil record. Were it not for this extraterrestrial invader, the small and inconspicuous warm-blooded mammals would likely have remained dwarfs. Nature's experiment with larger (and therefore more conspicuous) mammals would have soon become a quick snack for the predominant dinosaur. Dinosaur extinction allowed mammals to grow in size. We can be grateful for this demarcation line in the fossil record. Otherwise, in our vain elderly years, we would likely strive to maintain that fresh, youthful, cold, clammy reptilian look.

At about 11:59 p.m. creatures resembling a chimpanzee stood about four to five feet tall with bones similar to ours and with one half our brain volume. At 48 seconds to midnight *Homo habilis* (dextrous man) appeared. At 31 seconds to midnight, *Homo erectus* (erect man) arrived. There's a notable difference between *Homo habilis* and *Homo erectus*. If *Homo erectus* sought admission to a Museum of Natural History, he might appear to be a wearisome patron, but his admission fee could reasonably be accepted. If *Homo habilis* tried to gain entry, he would likely be ushered to an exhibit booth on a more permanent basis.

Homo sapiens sapiens (humans indistinguishable from us) arrived less than one second before midnight.[51]

---

[51] G. Tyler Miller, Jr., *Living in the Environment*, Wadsworth Publishing Company, 1994; William K Hartmann & Ron Miller, *The History of Earth*, Workman Publishing, 1991.

Civilization, as we know it, would represent about one-tenth of a second. This can't even be measured by a finger snap. A camera flashbulb illuminates more time than the entire span of recorded civilization. A mere fleeting moment. This we call history.

We plod through life with a sense of time driven by celestial movements and seasonal changes. We pace ourselves with the unalloyed certainty of sunup following sundown and the austerity of winter followed by the lushness of spring. Our biological clock are set to nature's pulsations and we regulate ourselves accordingly.

Environmental change is governed by a different clock. Degradation does not occur during the interval from sunup to sundown. Toxic landfills do not reach the threatening levels from one season to the next. Our biological clocks step to the beat of a different drummer.

We are genetically hard-wired to nature's cadence. Temperatures and weather patterns from one season to the next impart profound change in our lives. Yet seasonal swings represent a mere quiver on the clock of environmental harm. This harm can become imperceptible to our biological level of consciousness.

It is only by collapsing the course of the Earth's history into a comprehensible time frame that we can begin to appreciate the magnitude of our destructive potential. The time period between World War II and the present is scarcely measurable in contrast with the 4.5 billion year history of the planet. Yet, during this brief interval, forests have retreated by human intervention, CO_2 gases have proliferated, non-biodegradable products of chemistry clutter virgin mountain tops and untraversed ocean floors, life's protective ozone shield has been compromised, and artificial lights emblazon the night sky across the industrialized world.

We prefer to believe our intellect enables us to avert harm. The harsh reality of exponential growth, however, cooperates with human biorhythms to render us ill-equipped to perceive environmental and population risks. Our probationary seat at the top of the food chain only describes the depth of a fall due to environmental degradation. This lofty perch does little to improve our vantage and ability to foresee impending hazards.

A conservation ethic requires us to take the long view and escape the constraints of our biological clocks. Historic images of the world around us shed light on our destructive potential. Population pressures are taking us to still unknown destinations. And we are proceeding at a fearsome and unsustainable pace. In the word selected by Lindsey Grant, it's a "Juggernaut."

11

THE HUMAN JUGGERNAUT

Famine seems to be the last, the most dreadful resource of nature. The power of population is so superior to the power in the earth to produce subsistence for man, that premature death must in some shape or other visit the human race. The vices of mankind are active and able ministers of depopulation. They are the precursors in the great army of destruction, and often finish the dreadful work themselves. But should they fail in this war of extermination, sickly seasons, epidemics, pestilence, and plague, advance in terrific array, and sweep off their thousands and ten thousands. Should success be still incomplete, gigantic, inevitable famine stalks in the rear, and with one mighty blow, levels the population with the food of the world.
— Malthus, 1798, Chapter VII

THE QUEST FOR a metaphor on population issues has settled on the word Juggernaut.[52] In southern India, the Juggernaut is a large ceremonial chariot used in religious festivals. The unwieldy chariot is pushed and pulled with god-fearing fervor, but it is not controllable. It damages whatever falls in its path; mineral, vegetable, animal, or human. Survival and safety become a matter of random fate.

Population, like the Juggernaut, also bears a fearsome quality, but population is propelled by a different force; human indifference. An indifference to limits. A purely Malthusian quality. By suppressing reality, the population Juggernaut remains fixed on its destructive course unless foresight and human compassion conspire against it.

---

[52] Lindsey Grant, *Juggernaut*, Seven Locks Press, 1996.

We are long overdue for a call to arms against the basic environmental threat: population. Why has this issue lost its claim to the American conscience? Why was population the primary issue on Earth Day 1970 and a forgotten cause on Earth Day in the more heavily populated 1990s? Why do major environmental groups flee from immigration reform? How did discussions on fertility rates become a political taboo? Why has funding for family planning subsided? Is there no longer a legitimate population issue? Have natural resources expanded? Will pollution sinks generously continue to accommodate our excesses? How does an issue like population vanish from the agenda?

First, and perhaps foremost, the abortion issue is, in many circles, a moral absolute. Once population is on the table, it inevitably becomes entangled with the abortion debate. Passions rage. Impetuosity and faith trump reason. Politicians seek shelter. Rather than imperil a friendship or threaten a political alliance, it's safer to dodge the population issue. Does deafening silence remove the risk?

Other explanations for our present disregard of population issues include universalism (the one-world dream which conveniently overlooks any obligation we may have to the environment and to America's disenfranchised), innumeracy (the mathematical equivalent of illiteracy), the failure of leadership, a denial of reality, an unexamined allegiance to growth, the birth control debate and claims of racism in the immigration debate. These issues have operated to suppress the population issue as a matter of concern.

Whether you are concerned about conservation, freedom, independence, standard of living, racial equality, feminism, education, democracy, jobs, opportunities, migration, compassion or even biblical directives, population is your cause. It resides at the heart of your discontent. Nevertheless, we remain mired in mental paralysis on this foundational topic.

As we ascend to awesome heights on an exponential population curve, we increasingly deplete resources and add to pollution, yet America's public policy opens a wider door to high fertility immigrants. This imposes additional pressures on dwindling resources and steadily contributes to mounting wastes. We're on a cycle. A treadmill.

Synergies (forces driving each other) spiral out of control. More consumption. A bigger magnet for migration. More waste. More people. Yet talk of population remains suppressed.

The population and immigration debate is not a let's-feel-good-about-ourselves issue. Yet, beneath the veneer of bleak scenarios there can be a sense of untiring hope for the future.

Malthus endured criticism as a dispassionate prophet of doom and gloom. Yet, history may vindicate him as the compassionate visionary with steadfast hope for mankind. Will future historians similarly see compassion and altruism in today's advocates of population policies?

ILLUSIONS FROM INDIA

And, the superior power of population cannot be checked without introducing misery or vice, the ample portion of these too bitter ingredients in the cup of human life, and the continuance of the physical causes that seem to have produced them, bear too convincing a testimony.
— Malthus, 1798, Chapter II

W E PREFER TO see the world as a place compatible with human life. Whether it is a matter of manifest destiny, illusions of grandeur, biblical mandates or inalienable rights, we tend to resist any suggestion that an ever-expanding abundance of human life might be detrimental.

As previously indicated, in the 1950s, there was a worldwide annual net population gain (births minus deaths) of approximately 50 million. In the 1960s, it was 60 million per year. The 1970s had 70 million, the 1980s had 80 million, and the third millennium could see net population gains of 100 million per year. Yet prolific life is still avidly embraced in many quarters.

In 1993, an earthquake in India killed 30,000 people. This story became international headline news. Yet, there were no newscasts on why this disaster really occurred. It's as though there was a conspiracy of silence on why 30,000 people in India were living on the edge of a potential earthquake.

News reporters speedily announced the discernible cause of the disaster. They reported it was the earthquake. No question. The earth quaked and the loss of life followed. First a quake. Then death. Quakes cause death. B follows A. Therefore, A causes B. Could this be a logical fallacy?

Was population mentioned as a cause? Did fertility rates become part of the story? Would the public have sensed a mean-spirited cheerlessness if population projections were part of the story?

The cruel and painful reality is that India, an already heavily overpopulated nation, had a daily net population gain of 50,000 people! That's right, 50,000 more births than deaths every day.[53] The calamitous loss of 30,000 lives was replenished by India's surging demographics in less than two eight hour work shifts.

Maybe it is not necessary for the news headlines to say: "India Replenishes its Tragic Loss of Life to an Earthquake by the Time this Breaking Headline Reaches You." Perhaps there's a tactful and sensitive way to incorporate this information in the interest of disseminating "news." In the case of India, there's only one reason people were living in the earthquake zone. That is population. There's no place else to go. And, lest our successors see us as unthinking beings, there should be a level of congeniality and tolerance for population information among the news readership.

Garrett Hardin has, for years, questioned the ethics of contributing food to countries having exceeded the carrying capacity of their land mass. As populations surge, the quantity of suffering increases exponentially. Unless the pledge of food is accompanied with a promise to provide unlimited quantities of food for an ever-growing population, it becomes a cruel hoax. Syndicated columnist Georgie Anne Geyer speaks of her meeting with Garrett Hardin in *Americans No More:*

> When we had lunch in Washington two years later, my first impression of Hardin--a professor emeritus of the University of California at Santa Barbara accused of being "nativist, bigoted, and xenophobic"--was that he was such a gentleman. A courtly man, then in his eighties, who moves carefully with a walker, a brilliant scientist filled with a youthful, effervescent joy in life, he is far from the "hate-monger" portrayed by pro-immigration types. . . . The Socratic Mr. Hardin then leaned across the table and asked me, "Let us grant ourselves the

[53] John H. Tanton, M.D., "End of the Migration Epoch," *The Social Contract*, Vol. IV, No. 3, Spring, 1994.

most malevolent of motives: Let us ask, `How can we harm India--*really harm her?*' Quite simply, by sending India a bounty of food, year after year."[54]

Somalia has touched the world's heart strings with graphic photographs of starvation. We responded with massive airlifts of food and even military support as long as images of hardship were carried by our nightly news. The duration of this costly response bore a striking relationship to the attention span of the basic TV addict. In our swift and short-lived response, did we ever consider the root cause of Somalia's problem? According to the Population Reference Bureau of Washington DC the average Somalian woman has 6.6 children. This is exactly twice the worldwide average of 3.3 children per woman. This fertility rate adds 240,000 extra mouths to Somalia's hungry table every year, or a net increase of 657 per day! This occurs in a country with donated food grains as its major import and graphic photographs of hunger as its major export.[55]

If there were insufficient resources to feed Somalia's 8.3 million in 1992 before the massive aid program, then how will its projected 13.9 million inhabitants be fed in 2010? How many cases of starvation would there be today if our 1980 aid could have enabled Somalia's population to then stabilize at 6.7 million? Have we victimized Somalia with our compassionate, but short-term, solutions? Have we overlooked the harsh reality of finite resources on a finite planet with exponential population growth?

If we are unable to responsibly digest the cold hard facts of population, then Pogo's admonition will become a self-fulfilling prophecy: "We have met the enemy and he is us." We can become both predator and prey. The hunter becomes the hunted.

There's much to be learned from peering in the eyes of our non-human companions. Small mammals scampering about on the forest

---

[54] Georgie Anne Geyer, *Americans No More*, The Atlantic Monthly Press, 1996, pp. 269, 270.

[55] John F. Rohe, Somalia and the Overpopulation Connection, *Focus*, Carrying Capacity Network, Volume 3, No. 1, 1993.

floor become prey for animals perched upon a higher niche in the food chain. Mice and voles fall in this category. They are on constant alert of the ever-present predator. By Darwinian experiment, they keep an eye peeled over their shoulder. Accordingly, their eyes are positioned on the sides of their head.

The predator, on the other hand, has eyes in front. No need to maintain a rear guard. The predator's competitive advantage is derived from maintaining a constant focus on the prey where it is. In front.

The owl is a prime predator. Near the top of the food chain, it is a formidable opponent of any mouse or vole. It is swift, sleek and silent. Equipped with sharp talons, it is mercifully abrupt in quenching life from its prey. Night vision and eyes directly in front enable the owl to become a well focused gaze on wings.

When we look in a mirror, we'll similarly find eyes in front peering back into our own. As we glance ahead, we might conclude these are the eyes of a predator. Focused, our eyes are in front. We are perched at a lofty height in the food chain.

But we're not alone. The mirror image also has eyes in front, focused vision, and can maintain an equally stern gaze. It takes a split second for light to travel from us to the mirror and to be reflected back. Yet in this brief, abstract interval, the image becomes inverted. As a "mirror image," our right becomes left in the mirror. And the mirror's left is our right. A mirror image of this page would read backwards, from your right to left.

Could our reflected and inverted image with eyes in front be that of a focused predator peering back at its prey? Is the hunter now the hunted? Does our human compassion for the tragic loss of life to an earthquake in India stifle our ability to responsibly address the true cause? Are we blinded by compassion? How can we avert a similar disaster in the future? Will dreadful casualties from population excesses be our destiny? Have we become both predator and prey?

The early Romans had a phrase for this: *homo homini lupus* ("man is a wolf to man").[56]

---

[56] Adapted from the play *Asinaria* by Plautus. See Eugene Ehrlich, Amo, Amas, Amat and More, Harper & Row Publishers, Inc., 1985, p. 144.

The indifference to limits inflicts punishment upon the unfortunate. Those finding it necessary to live in a hazardous setting, because there's no where else to go, now bear the brunt of the decision to not responsibly address the population issue. As available food sources are contrasted with burgeoning human numbers, the Malthusian crunch will be unwittingly imposed on the innocent.

13

FOOD CHAIN

The germs of existence contained in this spot of earth, with ample food and ample room to expand, would fill millions of worlds in the course of a few thousand years. Necessity, that imperious all pervading law of nature, restrains them within the prescribed bounds. The race of plants and the race of animals shrink under this great restrictive law. And the race of man cannot, by any efforts of reason, escape from it. Among plants and animals its effects are waste of seed, sickness, and premature death. Among mankind, misery and vice.
— Malthus, 1798, Chapter I

THERE'S GOOD NEWS and bad news for consumers of food. The good news is that food production continues to increase. The bad news is that the production of people is increasing even faster.

For most of our industrial history, food production increased faster than human populations. Diets improved. People generally became healthier. Nutritional deficiencies were eliminated. Near the end of the 20th century this changed. Population increases are now out-pacing agricultural gains.

With scientifically engineered hybrids, inorganic fertilizers, pesticides, herbicides, irrigation, and efforts to stabilize soils, present harvests are continuing to increase. Between 1984 and 1993, however, world grain production has dropped 12% per person. Similarly, seafood, beef and mutton production for each person on the globe has dropped.[57] These

---

[57] Lester Brown and Hal Kane, *Full House*, W.W. Norton & Co., 1994, p. 22. U.S. Dept. Agriculture (USDA), Economic Research Service (ERS) "World Grain Database" (unpublished printout, Washington, D.C., 1992).

"per person" figures say more about surging human population growth than about modest increases in agricultural production. In other words, any increase in agricultural harvests is now dwarfed by the extra quarter-million mouths added to the banquet table every day.

This probably has not yet been reflected in the quantity of cereal in your morning bowl. If, unlike many farm workers in the Third World, you have spare time to be reading this, it might take a while for these per capita shortages to be visited upon your household. The effects of "per capita" shortages will be more poignant in the Third World where the majority of earnings are allocated toward a family's subsistence provisions.

Trends can illuminate the future.

The Malthusian food shortage is now unfolding worldwide, but it is likely to take a while before this is reflected in the American diet.

Even utopians are now beginning to ponder future shortages. Gregg Easterbrook is commonly associated with the optimistic brownlash movement.[58] The notion of limits has even crept into his writings on agronomist Norman Borlaug:

> Like most agronomists, Borlaug has always advocated using organic fertilizers - usually manure - to restore soil nutrients. But the way to attain large quantities of manure is to have large herds of livestock, busily consuming the grain that would otherwise feed people. Inorganic fertilizers based on petroleum and other minerals can renew soil on a global scale - at least as long as the petroleum holds out.[59]

Well, OK, but while fossil fuels continue to be drained, the population continues to surge. Garrett Hardin would challenge: "And

---

[58] Paul R. Ehrlich and Anne H. Ehrlich, *Betrayal of Science and Reason*, Island Press, 1996. The "brownlash movement" is the backlash to the green environmental movement.

[59] Gregg Easterbrook, Forgotten Benefactor of Humanity, *Atlantic Monthly*, January, 1997.

then what?"[60] You will not find a satisfactory response among those indifferent to limits. Is it prudent to hand these challenges to our successors while, for now, the numbers spiral?

At present, China relies primarily on grains in its diet. But a change is afoot. In 1993, a Chinese villager saw an improvement in his lifestyle: "Overall, life has gotten much better. My family eats meat maybe 4 or 5 times a week now. Ten years ago, we never had meat."[61] Moving into a meat and poultry diet means the grains first move through the animals before the animals are consumed by people. This is a less efficient use of grain.

Highly prolific poultry requires two pounds of grain for each pound of meat.[62] Pigs are less prolific, and less efficient. Four units of grain translates into one unit of pork.[63] Beef production is still less efficient. Seven units of grain produce one unit of beef.[64] As the Chinese economy grows, it can be expected to eat higher on the food chain. More grain will be required to meet expectations of the ever-increasing Chinese population.

Advances on the food chain are costly investments not only for humans, but also for other forms of life. For example, weight gain in aquatic animal systems increases at 10% from one level in the food chain to the next. Jerry Dennis, author of *The Bird in the Waterfall*, describes the process as follows:

---

[60] Garrett Hardin, *Living Within Limits*, Oxford University Press, 1993.

[61] Nicholas D. Christoff, "Riddle of China: Repression as Standard of Living Soars" *New York Times*, Sept. 7, 1993.

[62] Robert V. Bishop et al, *The World Poultry Market - Government Intervention and Multilateral Policy Reform* , (Washington D.C.: USDA, 1990).

[63] Leland Southard, *Livestock and Poultry Situation and Outlook Staff*, ERS, USDA, Washington, D.C., cited as a private communication, April 27, 1992, in Brown, Lester, R. *Who Will Feed China?* W.W. Norton & Co., 1995, Chapter 3, fn. 10.

[64] Allen Baker, *Feed Situation and Outlook Staff*, ERS, USDA, Washington, D.C. cited as a private communication, April 27, 1992, in Brown, Lester, R. *Who Will Feed China?* W.W. Norton & Co., 1995, Chapter 3, fn. 10.

On average, the transfer of energy from one level to the next is only 10 percent efficient. For a shark or killer whale at the top of the pyramid to gain 1 pound in body weight it must eat 10 pounds of third-level carnivore such as coho salmon. For a salmon to reach 10 pounds, it has to consume 100 pounds of baitfish. That 100 pounds of baitfish reached maturity only after eating 1,000 pounds of carnivorous zooplankton. The carnivorous zooplankton captured and ingested 10,000 pounds of herbivorous zooplankton which in turn devoured 100,000 pounds of phytoplankton. Many thousands of pounds of organisms must be consumed to produce every pound of top carnivore swimming in the ocean.[65]

In 1990, the average Chinese person consumed 100 eggs per year. By the year 2000, the official Chinese goal for egg consumption is 200 per person. If, on average, each of the anticipated 1.3 billion Chinese consume 200 eggs in the year 2000, then an additional 24 million tons of grain will be required for egg production. This is equal to the total annual Canadian grain exports. And Canada is presently the world's second highest grain exporter.[66]

If the Chinese diet moves up the food chain by expanding into milk, cheese, meat and other animal products, then the worldwide grain production needed just for China—never mind the other three-quarters of the world population—will impose an impossible demand on international grain exporters. A shortage of grains now donated to the needy is likely to become particularly acute.

How will the Chinese claim to worldwide grain affect the millions receiving food aid? How will this impact the occupants of nations in which the carrying capacity has been steadily overburdened with population excesses? Will civility reign supreme?

---

[65] Jerry Dennis, Glenn Wolff, *The Bird in the Waterfall*, Harper Collins Publishers, 1996, p. 229.

[66] U.S. Dept. of Agriculture (USDA), Economic Research Service (ERS), "Livestock and Poultry: World Markets and Trade," Washington, D.C., October, 1994, in Brown, Lester, R., *Who Will Feed China?*, W.W. Norton & Co., 1995., p. 48.

The U.S. presently has 1.8 acres of arable farmland per person. This is sufficient to provide a nutritious and diverse diet. As population mounts, the volume of available farmland will diminish on a per capita basis. As a practical matter, the diversity of food, rather than the quantity, in our diet will first be compromised. A diverse diet requires 1.2 acres of arable land per person. With present immigration policies, the U.S. is expected to have .6 acres of arable land per person by 2050.[67]

If history becomes our guide, then there's nothing speculative about Malthusian predictions of "misery and vice." The African experience with population pressures and scarcity reveal that diminishing taxes, reduced police protection, lawlessness, governmental breakdown, anarchy, roving gangs and brute force will prevail over justice.[68] Is this the modern day version of the "misery and vice" spectacle? Are other consequences in store for those willing to take a gamble with scarcity?

Malthusian concern for "misery and vice" is reminiscent of Garrett Hardin's "Eleventh Commandment":

Thou shalt not transgress the carrying capacity.[69]

Just as Americans began striking a balance with nature by reducing their fertility rates, the elected officials began undermining these efforts with lax immigration policies. Population excesses from other nations found lenient immigration laws at the U.S. border. Other industrialized nations invested in technology and capital investments in preparation for the challenges of the 21st century. We, however, began investing in cheap foreign labor and the social problems caused by unemployment

---

[67] David Pimentel and Mario Giampietro, "Food, Land, Population, and the U.S. Economy," (Washington D.C.: Carrying Capacity Network, 1994); Virginia Abernethy, "The Politics of Conservation," *Focus*, Carrying Capacity Network, Vol. 7, No. 1, 1997, p. 26; "Why a 100,000 Limit on Immigration is Realistic and Necessary," *Focus*, Carrying Capacity Network, Vol 7, No. 1, 1997, p. 18.

[68] Robert Kaplan, "The Coming Anarchy," *Atlantic Monthly*, March, 1994.

[69] Garrett Hardin, *Living Within Limits*, Oxford University Press, 1993, p. 207.

of our underprivileged.[70] These policies bespeak an indifference to limits on the frontiers of employment, resources and of the public treasury.

---

[70] Paul Kennedy, *Preparing for the Twenty-First Century,* Random House, 1993.

14

BORDERING ON INDIFFERENCE

The advocate for the perfectibility of man, and of society, retorts on the defender of establishments, a more equal contempt. He brands him as the slave of the most miserable and narrow prejudices, or as the defender of the abuses of civil society, only because he profits by them. He paints them either as a character who prostitutes his understanding to his interest; or as one whose powers of mind are not of a size to grasp anything great and noble, who cannot see above the five yards before him, and who must therefore be utterly unable to take in the views of the enlightened benefactor of mankind.
— Malthus, 1798, Chapter I

THE INDIFFERENCE TO limits is perhaps most conspicuous in the immigration debate.

It didn't create much of a stir. It hardly caught the attention of the media. It was just another number. And one of many that slipped into the massive mound of paperwork churned out from the government in 1992.

In 1989, the U.S. Census Bureau predicted U.S. population would peak in the year 2040 at 302 million. It would then plateau and begin to slowly fall. Just three years later, in 1992, the U.S. Census Bureau predicted the U.S. population would not peak at 302 million, but rather would grow to 383 million by the year 2050. And they still missed the mark. The 1992 numbers were based on the assumption that fertility and immigration rates would remain below the actual 1992 levels. These assumptions were wrong. If actual fertility and immigration rates are substituted for the erroneous assumptions, then by the year 2050 there will be 506 million Americans.[71] That's almost twice the number present in 1998, the Malthusian bicentennial! The miscalculations primarily resulted from the U.S. Census Bureau's failure or inability to tabulate the effect of immigration.

Since the publication of Paul Ehrlich's *Population Bomb* in 1968 and since Earth Day 1970, Americans have decided to take control of their demographic destiny, but government policies have been slow to follow. The baby boomers of the 1940s and 1950s opted for smaller families. Whether motivated by economic interests, the opportunity costs of child-bearing, college expenses or by environmental concerns, since 1970, the U.S. has generally experienced dwindling fertility rates. U.S. citizens have essentially attained a replacement level fertility. Demographers tell us this is 2.1 children per woman. (This isn't a chauvinistic number, it's just that since men do not give birth to children the demographers count only women in fertility rate statistics.)

According to U.S. Census data, the U.S. population in 1790 was about 4 million people. In the mid-1990s it was 256 million. That sounds like a big difference, but it is only six doublings of the 1790 population. In other words: 4, 8, 16, 32, 64, 128, 256. And current immigration policies will cause the number to again double by the middle of the 21st century.

Is there any realistic hope that our land could accommodate even one more doubling? That's twice as many sewer flushes, twice as many roads, homes, parking lots, malls, lost agricultural lands, landfills, wetland losses and contributions to the toxic waste stream. Current immigration policies have us heading there within the next century, notwithstanding this nation's conscientious decision to reduce its fertility on Earth Day 1970.

The number of working age people in industrial countries is now relatively stable, year after year.

The Third World, however, has nearly 3 billion working age people. Another 60 million working age people are added to the Third World

---

[71] Otis L. Graham, Jr., *A Limited Bounty*, McGraw-Hill, 1996, p. 302.

employment hopefuls every year.[72] How will the Third World find meaningful occupations for the 3 billion hopefuls? And how will they accommodate the extra 60 million new entrants every year?

In the next 18 years, the Third World will add over one billion new employment seekers. It is not necessary to predict fertility rates in the future for this statistic. The future employment hopefuls are already here. It is only a matter of time for their passage through youth. The one billion entrants to the Third World labor force is more than the total employment in more developed countries after several centuries of industrialization! In 1994 the total employment for more developed countries was 600 million.[73] How will the Third World create more new jobs in the next 18 years than the industrialized world has created in several hundred years of progress?

Employment seekers can be expected to increase migratory pressures. As the underprivileged in the U.S. search for work, they are jostled to the back of the job line by burgeoning immigrants and by employers seeking cheap labor. This undermines the social safety net (welfare, jobs and education) for our poor. The U.S. is unable to create adequate employment opportunities for its underprivileged. Yet we maintain lax immigration policies and remain resolutely indifferent to employment limits.

It takes time for a nation to control its demographic future. Replacement level fertility today will not cause the population to immediately stabilize. In fact, it would take approximately 60 years for the decisions of Earth Day 1970 to result in a stationary population.[74]

Paradoxically, just as 1970 Earth Day attendees were being influenced by Paul Ehrlich, Congress began implementing immigration policies causing the nation to exceed its biological and cultural carrying capacity. According to one of the nation's leading journalists, Georgie Anne

---

[72] Lindsey Grant, *Juggernaut*, Seven Locks Press, 1996, p. 133.

[73] John H. Tanton, M.D., "End of the Migration Epoch," *The Social Contract*, Vol. IV, No. 3, Spring, 1994.

[74] Roy Beck, *Re-Charting America's Future*, The Social Contract Press, 1994, see chart on the cover.

Geyer:

> Before, immigrants were expected to embrace American values;
> after 1965 (the year of extensive revisions to immigration laws),
> Americans were forced or felt they were being forced to adapt to
> foreign cultural values. Ironically, these were often the same
> cultural values that for centuries had caused hardship, misery, and
> conflict in the immigrants' home countries, had made it impossible
> for those poor lands to develop, and finally had forced people to
> flee to America.[75]

Over one-half of the post-1970 U.S. population growth has been
from immigrants arriving after 1970, and their descendants.[76] According
to Houston political scientist Donald Huddle and immigration specialist
David Simcox, between 1993 and 2002, immigration will cost the U.S.
668.5 billion dollars. That's over two-thirds of a trillion dollars.[77]

On a planet having a *daily* net population gain of 250,000 people,[78]
90% of which originates in Third World nations, there will be
increasing pressures on all developed nations, including the U.S. This
is the "push" factor in migration. The "pull" factor is welfare, medical
care, housing, jobs, political stability, low inflation, family members and
free education provided by the destination country.

Lax immigration policies on legal immigration, and feeble border
controls on illegal immigration, undermine the demographic hopes of
this nation. Prospects for a sustainable future, imparted by voluntarily

---

[75] Georgie Anne Geyer, *Americans No More*, Atlantic Monthly Press, 1996, p. 251.
See also Roy Beck, *The Case Against Immigration*, W.W. Norton & Co., 1996 and Peter
Brimelow, *Alien Nation*, Random House, 1995.

[76] Roy Beck, *Re-Charting America's Future*, The Social Contract Press, 1994.

[77] Georgie Anne Geyer, *Americans No More*, Atlantic Monthly Press, 1996, p. 263.
See also Roy Beck, *The Case Against Immigration*, W.W. Norton & Co., 1996.

[78] World Population Data Sheet, Population Reference Bureau, Washington, D.C.,
1997.

reduced fertility in the U.S., are thwarted by these policies.

Anyone planning to challenge this system should bring a thick skin. You can expect mind-numbing accusations of racism and mean-spirited motives to stifle prospects for a meaningful dialogue. Ironically, the open border proponents hoisting emotional charges of racism and malicious motives are often bankrolled by big business.[79] These interests are eager to capitalize on cheap foreign labor, while our workforce is either callously bumped to the back of the job line or caused to work for lower wages. Taxpayers are then handed the bill to resolve social problems resulting from low wages and growing unemployment.

Unless our frame of reference enables us to view the implications of present immigration policies in 50 or 70 years, then it is impossible to begin thinking of sustainability. The high number of legal and illegal immigrants (and their high fertility levels[80]) cause immigration to be the single most prominent factor affecting a balance between people and resources in the United States.[81]

The compassion and sensitivity with which we evaluate immigration numbers will substantially influence whether we can leave an undiminished and sustainable legacy. This will require us to make choices. Whether we acknowledge it or not, life's choices confront us. Explicitly or implicitly, the choice involves our views on duties to succeeding generations and to foreigners (those who migrate and the vastly larger number staying behind). Who is within our primary realm of altruism? Does everyone on earth have the same claim to our altruism as do close relatives? Do we benefit foreign nations by accepting their population excesses now? Or are they benefitted more

---

[79] Georgie Anne Geyer, *Americans No More*, The Atlantic Monthly Press, 1996; Roy Beck, *The Case Against Immigration*, W.W. Norton & Co., 1996 and Donald Huddle, Ph.D., *The Net Costs of Immigration: The Facts, the Trends, and the Critics, Carrying Capacity Network, 1996*.

[80] Virginia D. Abernethy, *Population Politics*, Insight Books, 1993.

[81] Leon F. Bouvier and Lindsey Grant, *How Many Americans?*, Sierra Club Books, 1994.

by appreciating the consequences of high fertility experiments sooner than later? Life compels decisions.

And when the dust settles on the immigration debate, are we likely to return to the Golden Rule?

15

THE GOLDEN RULE

It may at first appear strange, but I believe it is true, that I cannot by means of money raise a poor man and enable him to live much better than he did before, without proportionately depressing others in the same class. If I retrench the quantity of food consumed in my house, and give him what I have cut off, then I benefit him without depressing any but myself and family who, perhaps, may well be able to bear it.
—— Malthus, 1798, Chapter V

DISCUSSION OF IMMIGRATION issues prompts considerations of the needy in less developed nations. The issue is not whether we should serve with altruism. It's not whether we shall serve with compassion. Rather, the issue is how to act with altruism and compassion. Who we shall serve? To deny it is a matter of choice betrays the failure to acknowledge limits. It is an indifference to limits.

Maybe we have a duty to all persons at or below the Mexican *per capita* income. Since Mexico supplies more U.S. immigrants than any other country, this standard has logical appeal.[82]

There are 4.5 billion people in the world earning less than the average Mexican. If, in the interest of equality and compassion, we determine our immediate duty is to these 4.5 billion people, then how shall we respond to this duty? Should the U.S. simply open its borders? Should it add to the present U.S. population of 270 million until it attains the population density of, say, India? Somalia? Or should it just admit the immigrants who may best serve America's needs, thereby prompting a

---

[82] Roy Beck, *Immigration by the Numbers*, a video published by The Social Contract Press, 1996.

brain drain where these minds are needed most?

The sheer numbers are daunting. If America were to accept even a small fraction of the Third World population increase of some 80 million per year, the results would be catastrophic. If we can't responsibly cope with the present environmental problems, how can we justify compromising the nation's natural legacy further with such expansive immigration policies? Can this be justified under a banner of compassion? Compassion to whom? Who has a claim on our altruism? (It is tempting to answer everyone, everywhere, every time, for ever and ever, world without end, amen. But then, like utopian fools, we'll be leaving a legacy of destruction.)

Does America have a duty to plunder its present and to squander its hereafter? Is "future abuse" a moral necessity?

Any sense of duty or responsibility to surging populations elsewhere should be balanced against a sense of respect for one's own relatives, children and grandchildren. By what claim of right can we compromise their world? Particularly when an open borders policy does little more than open a safety valve on flaming populations. An open border does not respond to the cause of the fire. It even lowers the heat in high fertility nations and thus reduces the incentive to address the very cause of the problem. Does the radius of altruism extend to all people in other nations, or should it extend primarily to our successors?[83]

Just how does the Golden Rule operate in a world of 6 billion people?[84] St. Martin of Tours encountered a naked beggar on the road. He gave the beggar one-half of his cloak. Both derived a level of comfort and warmth. Is there a duty to tear the cloak in the global village?

Where the cloak can be torn in half and provide a measure of warmth to both you and the beggar, then tearing the cloak is the right thing to do. But what if there are 4.5 billion others seeking a piece of the cloak? What if they each advance the same moral claim to U.S.

---

[83] Garrett Hardin, *The Immigration Dilemma*, Federation for American Immigration Reform, 1995.

[84] Gerda Bikales, "The Golden Rule in the Global Village," *The Social Contract*, Winter, 1992-1993.

compassion as the average Mexican now piercing the southern border? Does the Golden Rule require the cloak to be shred into a billion worthless fragments? Just how does the Golden Rule operate in the global village?

The "nation of immigrants" argument might be the most common rhetorical reaction to immigration reform. We've always been a nation of immigrants, so how does one justify raising the draw bridge now? With the exception of a small plot in Ethiopia, every land is a nation of immigrants. Are border controls unjust everywhere? Furthermore, the U.S. has not always been a "nation of immigrants" to the extent we are today. Immigration has, in fact, traditionally been regulated. And it has been episodic. Immigration restrictions of 1924 enabled the nation to build the employment ranks of its underprivileged.[85] The "nation of immigrants" argument is also a product of an indifference to limits. It is nurtured by the historic belief that we can always solve our problems by migrating elsewhere. In fact, that's how problems were solved during the better part of our presence on earth. We could always find another land with deep rich soils, fresh sparkling waters and abundant minerals. There was invariably another frontier awaiting colonization. But, as John H. Tanton, M.D. ponders, what happens when we reach "the end of the migration epoch?"[86] Does the "nation of immigrants" argument still have relevance when there are just no longer available spaces with abundant resources awaiting colonization?

If only descendants of the native born have standing to assert immigration policies, then, as a practical matter, no one will ever assert border controls. Dan Stein, Executive Director of the Federation for American Immigration Reform, quips: To suggest that immigrants or their descendants cannot assert immigration controls is like suggesting that anyone who is the product of a full-term pregnancy cannot be pro-choice.

We may also derive guidance on the application of the Golden Rule

---

[85] Roy Beck, *The Case Against Immigration*, W.W. Norton & Co., 1996.

[86] John H. Tanton, M.D., "End of the Migration Epoch", *The Social Contract*, Vol. IV, No. 3, Spring, 1994.

from the Pope. The headquarters of the Roman Catholic Church, the Vatican, is a nation. This nation perhaps has the most restrictive of all immigration laws. The Pope will promote open borders when visiting New York (with four times the population density of the Vatican), yet he will return to the safe harbor of the Vatican after this mission of good will.[87]

Immigration issues require us to balance people against natural resources. Where are the ancient forests in your neighborhood beckoning to be cleared? Where is the biodiversity too well protected for future generations? Where are the waters too pure and lucid? Where is the unimpaired night sky too awe-inspiring? Where is there too little pavement? Where is there not enough urban sprawl? Where are the landfills too empty? Where is the air too fresh?

Immigration reform presents us with hard decisions. A person's country of origin has an investment in their upbringing, their medical care, and education. Our sincere compassion can best be expressed by enabling them to assist the nation having made this investment. Any dollars used to subsidize those who "cut and run" cannot be contributed to the needy left behind. And there is plenty of room for heartfelt compassion in helping others contribute directly to the country of their birth.

The Third World population explosion is not, however, the sole cause of harm. It would betray an indifference to limits were we to focus exclusively on burgeoning human numbers abroad without considering the excessive consumption and economic growth of first world countries. Ergo, the following Part Three addresses root causes of excess consumption.

---

[87] James S. Robb, "How Many Immigrants Does Vatican City Take? Actually, None.," *The Social Contract*, Vol. V, No. 4, Summer, 1995.

Part Three

ECONOMIC GROWTH

16

BASIC ECONOMICS

No limits whatever are placed to the productions of the earth; they may increase for ever and be greater than any assignable quantity; yet still the power of population being a power of a superior order, the increase of the human species can only be kept commensurate to the increase of the means of subsistence by the constant operation of the strong law of necessity acting as a check upon the greater power.
— Malthus, 1798, Chapter II

In 1798 Thomas Robert Malthus expressed anxiety over the indifference to limits. Were he writing today, he would be alarmed by the prevalent addiction to growth in a field now clinging to optimism. He would likely dwell on economics.

Maybe you saw it in your high school text. It was in the chapter on economics and business. It depicted the economic flow chart.

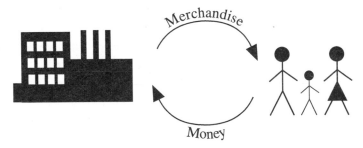

FIGURE 4. ECONOMIC FLOW CHART

Buildings representing manufacturers and sellers were shown on the left. People, the consumers, were on the right. A semi-circular arrow from the manufacturers to the consumers registered the passage of merchandise. Another arrow, from the consumers to the manufacturers, represented the transfer of money.

The economic flow chart taught us how the complete system functioned. Somebody manufactured something. And someone else bought it. Money changed hands. The flow of money tracked the passage of products and "better-offness" in this never-ending cycle.

Better-offness had nothing to do with the quantum of thoughtfulness projected on our successors. It was not a gauge of civic responsibility; of honoring our past or recognizing our future. It was just the pulse of self-indulgence.

It was bedrock, basic economics. Being "better off" meant more stuff was passing from the manufacturers to the consumers, and correspondingly more money was exchanged. The economic flow chart made good sense to us then. And it still makes sense to much of the business community today.

The economic flow chart also depicted economic growth. Larger or faster moving arrows demonstrated growth. Economic growth means the flow of products and money is spiraling upward at an ever increasing rate. Being "better off" means more economic growth and faster flows on the economic flow chart.

This basic economic flow chart illustrates the economist's view of the world. In a nutshell, it is the complete economic universe. Any effort to complicate the illustration will be vigorously opposed by the economic community.

Economic growth is touted as a virtue in every business report. It would be heretical to even question the premise that growth is good and more growth is better. Growth leads to prosperity. It leads to "better off-ness." And it is harmlessly depicted in the economic flow chart.

But the flow chart is an oversimplification. It fails to consider entropy.

17

ENTROPY

These facts prove the superior power of population to the means of subsistence in nations of hunters, and that this power always shows itself the moment it is left to act with freedom.

It remains to inquire whether this power can be checked, and its effects kept equal to the means of subsistence, without vice or misery.
— Malthus, 1798, Chapter III

HERE'S A SCARY thought: Thermodynamics!

This word has struck terror into the hearts of college students everywhere. During registration, the mere sight of a Thermodynamics curriculum has caused students to seek intellectual refuge elsewhere. They fled to the schools of business and finance and successfully evaded information on the second law of Thermodynamics.

Stripped of its trappings, here's a mercifully brief explanation of the second law of thermodynamics. Consider your kitchen or bedroom. If you do not apply energy to maintain its cleanliness, it proceeds from a state of order to disorder over time. Dishes mount in the sink, the surrounding counter top, and eventually engulf the kitchen. Similarly, the barrage of dirty laundry will eventually overwhelm your bedroom. That's the second law. A system, when subjected to use, proceeds from a state of order to disorder. That's it. Nothing more. It's the second law.

Entropy is a measure of the disorder in a system. In other words, your kitchen and bedroom started with low entropy. That is, it was highly organized. As it was used, the room moved from the state of order to disorder. It became high in entropy. When we use something in a system, over time it moves from low entropy to high entropy.

The second law and entropy explain why the economic flow chart is a colossal over-simplification.

18

ECONOMICS RE-EXAMINED

Suppose, that by a subscription of the rich, the eighteen pence a day which men earn now was made up five shillings; it might be imagined, perhaps, that they would then be able to live comfortably, and have a piece of meat every day for their dinners. But this would be a very false conclusion. The transfer of three shillings and sixpence a day to every labourer would not increase the quantity of meat in the country.
— Malthus, 1798, Chapter V

T HEY NEVER TAUGHT us the economic flow chart was simple-minded. We learned it was just a matter of manufacturers making "stuff" that made us "better off" for which we exchanged money. The more stuff and money, the more better off we should have become. More economic growth meant more happiness. This pleases the purveyors of stuff and it tends to get politicians elected.

But there's a conspiracy of silence. Or maybe the economists were too timid to venture into the second law of Thermodynamics. Here's how Thermodynamics applies to the basic economic flow chart.

The economic flow chart does not reveal "throughput." It is like a picture of a faucet and sink, with no water. It is akin to the illustration of an animal with no digestive tract. It is like a river bed with no rippling current.

"Throughput" refers to the material flow in the economic system. Resources (petroleum, metals, trees, open space, etc.) are withdrawn at one end of the system. These are then reconstituted, fabricated, paved over, assembled and packaged for sale. Then, for an interval, they become the source of "better off-ness" for the consumer. Eventually, the items become functionally or aesthetically obsolete and are then thrown away.[88]

Throughput is withdrawn from a "source" and eventually discarded in a "sink." It moves from source to sink while driving the cycle in the economic flow chart. Economic growth means more throughput. In other words, growth results in more aggressive withdrawal of resources and, eventually in a faster rate of disposal in the sink. It's the economic beast with bigger jaws and a higher rate of metabolism.

The second law of Thermodynamics governs throughput. Like the kitchen or bedroom when subjected to use, this system moves from a state of order to disorder. Petroleum, for example, represents the orderly arrangement of molecular structures developed hundreds of millions of years ago by photosynthetic processes. Stored safely in the earth's caverns, petroleum retained its organized state over the ages. We derive energy by burning this highly organized molecular structure. The remnants are not, however, quite so well organized. Petroleum moves from low entropy to high entropy as we harness its stored energy. It moves from a state of order to disorder. The "sink" for petroleum is the atmosphere. Greenhouse gases, such as CO_2, and other pollutants, become the disordered remnants of this primeval photosynthetic process. They have less order and a lower energy state.

Degraded sources and sinks, high in entropy, now proliferate. "Sources" are today represented by unsightly strip mines, dwindling water resources, depleted fish stocks, extinct or endangered species and in clear-cuts. "Sinks" are found in atmospheric pollution, greenhouse gases, contaminated ground water, and in toxic waste sites. These are the high entropy mounting dishes and laundry in our planetary household.

Not all activity on the economic flow chart is dependent upon the depletion of resources and "throughput" as we know it. Some economic activity is not resource dependent at all. For example, the exchange of ideas involves only human neurotransmitters, not natural resources. In the business of ideas, there is room for expansive, if not

---

[88] But what, as Garrett Hardin asks, will we do when there's no longer an away to which we can throw? Garrett Hardin, *Living Within Limits*, Oxford University Press, 1993, p. 201.

unlimited, growth. Limits in this realm are defined only by the outer boundary of our ingenuity.

If we had an economic system run entirely by neurological mental impulses, there would be no environmental degradation. But that's not how the system works. Every economic unit of exchange for an idea confers buying power upon the idea's owner. Buying power is commonly exercised by purchasing more stuff. More cars. More jet skis. That means acquiring a larger slice of the throughput. And throughput, inevitably, will eventually increase in entropy. It is then destined for the "sink."

The economic flow chart would more accurately be illustrated as a dependent part, a subsystem, of the surrounding ecosystem.

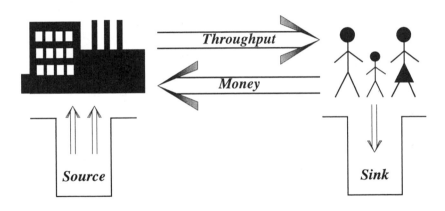

FIGURE 5. ECONOMIC FLOW CHART WITHIN THE ECOSYSTEM

Economics rely on a healthy ecosystem. Stated differently, there is less economy in a depleted and degraded ecosystem. High entropy means low economic security.

The arrows between the producers and the consumers in the economic flow chart should be shown as augers. Envision the spinning auger winding into a valued ecosystem. It augers into the earth. Economic growth assures the auger spins at an ever increasing rate. Throughput and disorder (high entropy) result from the process. Landfills and the atmosphere become the eventual sinks for our toxins and our discarded heat.

Alternatively, the economic flow chart can be depicted within an egg timer. As the flow chart arrows spin, grains of sand are passed from the top (the environmental "source") and into the bottom (the environmental "sink"). The grains of sand can again be elevated by photosynthesis, but there is still a problem with balance. We now disruptively affect the balance by harnessing low entropy fossil fuels and nuclear energy.

FIGURE 6. THE EGG TIMER

As long as throughput remains concealed from view, it will appear as though there's no environmental cost in the oversimplified flow chart. We will not appreciate the destructive force of this economic machine unless we confront it directly. Suppressing the effects of throughput numbs our perception and increases our feeling of security.

Suppression in America has moved beyond the growth advocates' expectations. It is now a constitutional principle. In 1992, the U.S. Supreme Court ruled one state could not reject another state's solid waste under the Commerce Clause of the U.S. Constitution. In other words, a state cannot reject foreign garbage. This may come as good news for states in the business of generating high volumes of garbage, but philosophically opposed to living near a landfill. However it's bad news for other states trying to responsibly manage their waste stream.

A society can reveal its sensitivity to limits in its attitude toward waste. Does it believe waste can truly be discarded? Is there a recognition that it will eventually be in someone's backyard? Or does it believe we can truly rid ourselves of it by sending it far enough away?

Instead of encouraging each state to responsibly deal with its throughput creations, the Commerce Clause now prohibits one state from refusing the solid waste of other states.[89] There are no rewards for states managing their own solid waste stream. Rather, they are now saddled with the waste of others. If we were serious about minimizing the waste stream, wouldn't we give each state the incentive to resolve its own solid waste problems? And if a state is unable to cope, then the market will establish a price point at which other states would be willing to accept their mess. Instead, trash now has something in common with race and religion: discrimination is prohibited.

The Supreme Court's decision is reminiscent of the *Saturday Night Live* solution to the solid waste crisis: The Yard-a-Pult. Erected in your backyard, it hurls your solid waste elsewhere. It is particularly useful for people not morally opposed to the principle of trashing the planet, but just put off by their proximity to the principle. The Yard-a-Pult is a

---

[89] *Fort Gratiot Sanitary Landfill, Inc. v Michigan Dept. of Natural Resources*, 504 U.S. 353 (1992).

NIMBY's[90] dream,[91] and it's now a constitutional priority.

By championing the cause of economic growth, we satisfy short-term consumptive appetites, but leave a legacy of high entropy: bountiful landfills, polluted waters and toxic air. By concealing this mess from our view and by hurling it elsewhere, we suppress reality and heap dishonor upon our successors.

Not all growth is necessarily harmful. Growth, however, has become a goal in itself. We're now committed to growth for the sake of growth. In the words of Ed Abbey: "Growth for the sake of growth is the ideology of a cancer cell."[92] The issue is not one of growth, but rather of sustainability. Donella Meadows speaks of growth as a singular goal in *The Limits to Growth*[93]:

> Growth is a means, not an end. When it gets you to where you want to go, the sensible thing is to stop.

It will take a veritable revolution of thought to even bring the horizons of a "stable mode" into view for the economic community.

We actively conceal the waste stream from ourselves. And now we're also camouflaging a similar element in the gross national product. The GNP awaits definition, but first, let's drop in on the Nelsons.

---

[90] NIMBY is an acronym for those sensitive to limits only on their turf and insensitive to limits elsewhere. "Not In My Back Yard."

[91] Al Gore, *Earth in the Balance*, Houghton Mifflin Co., 1992, p. 157.

[92] James R. Hepworth and Gregory McNamee, *Resist Much Obey Little, Remembering Ed Abbey*, Sierra Club Books, 1996.

[93] Donella H. Meadows, Dennis L Meadows, Jorgen Randers, and William W. Behrens III, *The Limits to Growth*, Potomac Associates, New American Library, 1972.

19

THE GROSS NELSON PRODUCT

For it should be observed that there is a very striking and essential difference between believing an assertion which absolutely contradicts the most uniform experience, and an assertion which contradicts nothing, but is merely beyond the power of our present observation and knowledge.
— Malthus, 1798, Chapter XII

THE NELSONS ARE your typical American family. Mom, dad, two children, double income, striving to provide security, an educational fund, soccer and a family legacy for their children. Mr. Nelson's unfettered optimism has been a source of inspiration for the family, but sometimes it tests their patience.

Mr. & Mrs. Nelson's joint earnings consistently total $50,000 per year. They own a home subject to a mortgage, each owns a car, they have a canoe and the customary trappings of a middle-class family.

Three years ago, Mr. Nelson's $10,000 car was totaled in an accident.

Two years ago, their $100,000 home was destroyed by a flood.

Last year, their $300,000 commercial real estate was lost to a fire.

Notwithstanding a rough three years, the Nelsons are in good health, and, despite the setbacks, strive to maintain a robust sense of optimism. In order to uphold the family's spirits, Mr. Nelson followed the lead of the U.S. Government and developed a better way to assess the family circumstances. He calls it the "Gross Nelson Product" or "GNP." It is a measure of the Nelson's total economic activity.

Accordingly, Mr. Nelson computed the family income ($50,000) plus losses ($10,000) three years ago. It totaled $60,000. This was the Gross Nelson Product. Two years ago, the total income ($50,000) plus losses ($100,000) moved to $150,000 and last year the GNP became $50,000 income plus $300,000 losses, i.e., $350,000.

The GNP increased from $60,000 to $100,000 two years ago. That's a 67% increase and last year it moved from $100,000 to $350,000. That's a 350% increase!

It would be perverse to suggest the Nelsons' lives are steadily improving because the Gross Nelson Product growth increased from 67% to 350%. The Nelson's losses make them steadily worse off. Not better. If they lost everything in a single year, the "Gross Nelson Product" would surely be up, but they surely wouldn't.

The "Gross Nelson Product" only measures the total economic activity in the Nelson household. The plus, the minus, and anything in between has been added to the perverse mix.

20

THE GROSS NATIONAL PRODUCT

The original improvers of telescopes would probably think that as long as the size of the specula and the length of the tubes could be increased, the powers and advantages of the instrument would increase; but experience has since taught us that the smallness of the field, the deficiency of light, and the circumstance of the atmosphere being magnified, prevent the beneficial results that were to be expected from telescopes of extraordinary size and power.
— Malthus, 1798, Chapter XII

THE GROSS NATIONAL Product, like the Gross Nelson Product, is a relatively recent invention. We began to recognize the Gross National Product as a measure of economic health in 1940.[94] Growth in the GNP is not only considered a favorable development, but it has become compulsory. Lackluster GNP growth becomes a justification for criticizing the incumbent political administration and justifies dislodging them from office.

Since the GNP has become a measure of our economic health and well-being, let's look at the properties of this 1940s quantity.

The GNP includes the total products and services provided by the nation. It assumes all economic activity is a good thing. The value of homes constructed, cars manufactured, foods grown, roads built and infrastructure installed are factored into the GNP. From the economist's perspective, these items would generally be viewed as

---

[94] Herman E. Daly, *Beyond Growth*, Beacon Press, 1996, p. 115. Otis L. Graham, Jr., *A Limited Bounty*, McGraw-Hill, 1996.

carrying a positive value on a nation's ledger of wealth. But, like the Gross Nelson Product, the Gross National Product does not stop with the pluses. It is really just a measure of total economic activity.

As a measure of economic activity, the GNP also adds the negatives. For example, losses resulting form the catastrophic *Exxon Valdez* crude oil spill were added to the GNP. So was the clean-up cost. All added economic activity.

The GNP does not subtract the loss of wetlands, diminished air quality, depleted or contaminated ground waters, soil degradation, diminished water quality, loss of habitat, strip mines and other scars to the landscape. The activities having led to these losses were all enthusiastically counted toward the economist's and politician's increased GNP. But the GNP counters turn a deaf ear to the eventual, and inevitable, costs of reclaiming clean air, safe water and an hospitable landscape. Yet reclamation costs are added into the GNP when remediation efforts are undertaken.

If your psychic dividends are derived from the natural amenities around you rather than the short-lived self-gratification of consumerism, then you're not in the GNP equation. You're beyond the pale. The GNP actively discriminates against you. Smelling the wild flowers may be a worthy exercise for you, but it won't be recognized by the GNP.

A college professor once said we can learn more about someone by examining their assumptions than by studying their conclusions. The GNP enthusiasts assume we're somehow better off when the negatives are added to our illusions of well being.

Imagine the Nelsons at their dinner table. Mr. Nelson reflects on the past three years. He reports the Gross Nelson Product moved from $60,000 to $100,000 to $350,000 during the three-year period. Were he to suggest the family was better off as a result of this increase in the "Gross Nelson Product" they would likely have him committed! Yet, we tirelessly yearn for our economists and politicians to reassure us that our Gross National Product continues to grow at an ever accelerating pace. Statements landing Mr. Nelson in a sanatorium earn others a term in the White House.

21

WEALTH AND ILLTH

I see no way by which man can escape from the weight of this law which pervades all animated nature. No fancied equality, no agrarian regulations in their utmost extent, could remove the pressure of it even for a single century. And it appears, therefore, to be decisive against the possible existence of a society, all the members of which should live in ease, happiness, and comparative leisure, and feel no anxiety about providing the means of subsistence for themselves and families.
— Malthus, 1798, Chapter I

W HEN THE GNP was formulated in the 1940s, how did the economists overlook the negatives and add losses? If truth in labeling laws had been in effect, would they have been compelled to call it the Gross National Product Plus Losses (GNPPL)?

The GNP is not only a measure of our nation's wealth, but it can also quantify our illth. If all American forests were converted into pulpwood and 2 x 4's in a single year, the GNP would show signs of vitality, but we wouldn't. How did notions of wealth and illth become so intimately intertwined that any distinction between them is blurred by the GNP? Here are a few root causes.

First, as previously mentioned, the second law of Thermodynamics (moving a closed system from a state of order to disorder) eludes the economist. Now that our created states of disorder (high entropy) meet us at every turn (foul air, toxic ground waters, expanding landfills, disturbed natural habitats, ozone depletion, greenhouse effect) the inescapability of the second law presses upon us with greater urgency than it did in 1940.

Second, we tend to judge our predecessors by present standards. In

1940, America was still a bountiful nation with vast resources. The population was less than one-half the 1998 figures. Non-biodegradable plastics were not yet cluttering the landfills. There was no particular need to consider the devaluation of earthly assets, such as natural resources and environmental quality. These assets were in abundant and seemingly unlimited supply. It may be wrong to condemn the GNP formulators of 1940 with our present frame of reference. But it is also wrong, and treacherous, not to adapt the GNP to present reality.

Third, our notions of freedom have undergone a transformation over the past few hundred years. When the nation was founded, freedom referred to breaking the oppressive bonds of a foreign ruler. The euphoric sense of liberty and freedom was found in the experiment of self-governance and a democratic union. Prevalent aspirations for the common good held the experiment intact as we declared freedom from oppression. Freedom from tyranny. Freedom from a foreign ruler.

Today we use the same word, freedom, but in a different sense. It now refers to the "unencumbered self."[95] The individual, and individual rights, have eclipsed earlier notions of the common good and aspirations for a shared common destiny.

It is easier to ignore long term consequences to our successors and the common good if we are taught to live for today and dwell only on individual, unencumbered freedom. The freedom contemplated by our founders emanated from an experiment in democracy and from a secure dwelling place for civic virtue.

Fourth, the economic flow chart is in need of an overhaul. As previously indicated, the conventional economic flow chart simply shows a flow of manufactured merchandise from the manufacturers and sellers to the users and consumers in exchange for money. Economists cherish this image from Econ 101. Its deceptive simplicity enables the economist to conveniently overlook an essential component of the flow chart. "Throughput," the material taken from the environmental source, is manipulated and used for an interval, and

---

[95] Michael J. Sandel, *Democracy's Discontent,* Belknap Press, 1996, p. 108.

then discarded in the environmental sink in a state of high "entropy."[96]

The economic flow chart is made to look like an independent, free-standing system in the economics books. But in reality, it is merely a subsystem of another system, the ecosystem. It is just part of the web of life around us. It has become an integral part of our biodiverse heritage and now it has metastasized on a primeval legacy. The economic system still imposes upon the surrounding ecosystem. Yet we still blindly compute ecological degradation as a positive in our GNP formulation.

Conventional accounting systems require no modification. We already use depreciation schedules for man-made artifacts. We already have a column for revenue and another for costs. An overhaul of the systems is not needed. Rather, we need to muster the intellectual courage to responsibly confront the true costs of our economic activity. These losses should be reflected in the loss column and deducted from the GNP. This is known as "greening the GNP."[97]

The business community is consumed by its affinity for growth. It is a matter of growth for the sake of growth. Geometric growth in human numbers was a frightful proposition for Malthus in 1798. He was a reactionary. Similarly, today, conservationists are reacting to the business community's growth ethic because it fails to appreciate the surging force of doubling numbers. It is indifferent to limits.

At the Malthusian bicentennial the global economy is approximately four times as large as it was in 1950[98] and it is projected to again be five times as large by 2050.[99]

Our political candidates are subjected to irresistible pressures to embrace a pro-growth rhetoric. In his 1992 best seller on ecology and

---

[96] Measure of disorder in a system under the second law of thermodynamics.

[97] Herman E. Daly, *Beyond Growth*, Beacon Press, 1996, p. 88.

[98] Lester R. Brown, "Launching the Environmental Revolution," in Brown et al., *State of the World*, 1992, p. 183.

[99] Jessica Tuchman Matthews, "The Case for Reinventing Technology to Promote Sustainable Development," in Lerner, *Earth Summit*, p. 29.

the human spirit, Al Gore identifies the "single most powerful force behind what seemed to be irrational decisions":

> The hard truth is that our economic system is partially blind. It "sees" some things and not others. It carefully measures and keeps track of the value of those things most important to buyers and sellers, such as food, clothing, manufactured goods, work and, indeed, money itself. But its intricate calculations often completely ignore the value of other things that are harder to buy and sell: fresh water, clean air, the beauty of the mountains, the rich diversity of life in the forest, just to name a few. In fact, the partial blindness of our economic system is the single most powerful force behind what seem to be irrational decisions about the global environment.[100]

On October 9, 1996, incumbent vice-president Al Gore was engaged in a televised debate with challenger Jack Kemp. In this debate, Kemp urged 5% annual growth in the economy and, as previously indicated, he wanted to see the economy double in 14 years. Notwithstanding Gore's recognition of the "blindness" in our economic computations, he deferred to the prevailing political winds in this debate. Gore retorted: "We should double the rate of growth and we should double the size of the American economy." Can we really be expected to double what he previously characterized as "the single most powerful force behind ... irrational decisions about the global environment" for political expediency?

The growth rhetoric has claimed the vocabulary of anyone seeking to appease the U.S. voter. It is disheartening to find that even in the context of a "debate" elect-ability requires all to concur on the merits of growth for the sake of growth.

Mr. Nelson's and the economist's unwillingness to consider the true costs of economic activity betrays an indifference to limits. It leads to a hazardous focus on misleading calculations such as the GNP.

---

[100] Al Gore, *Earth in the Balance*, Houghton Mifflin Company, 1992, pp. 182-183.

It will be difficult to attain a balance with our natural surroundings as long as this myth is perpetuated. Does anyone seriously claim we can continue plundering our surroundings at an ever increasing rate indefinitely? Forever and ever? Without end? And at an ever increasing rate of growth? If the answer is "no," then who among us will sound the alarm while there's still time?

We are of a divided mind. We foster conflicting objectives, and remove ourselves from the conflict. We take pride in our natural resources and we also strive for economic growth. Growth, in many instances compromises the resource base. There is only one way to escape the dilemma: denial. We aggressively deny a conflict. We studiously suppress notions of sustainability when it might threaten an economic objective. As long as we leash our aspirations to economic growth, the consequences are carelessly ignored.

Greening the GNP requires us to strike a meaningful balance with our surroundings. In June, 1986, a research group from Stanford University attempted to calculate the percentage of photosynthesis on land available to humans. In other words, some sunlight is needed to regenerate a plant. The rest of plant life could be made available for animals (human and non-human) to use or consume. Sunlight, after all, is life's basic energy source on earth. So how much of the net sunlight product do we humans take from the land? The researchers estimated 41%. One species now harnesses 41% of the net photosynthetic product from the land. The other 59% is left for other animals. And if the human population doubles again in the 46 years following this 1986 research, we could reach 82%. Just one more doubling may place us at 164%. A modern day "Malthusian crunch."

If you think escape is possible with a space journey, then think about this. Can we build enough space ships to accommodate just the net *daily* population increase of 250,000 people[101] (total births, minus deaths)? And if the journey were feasible, who would you invite aboard your craft? The highly fertile? The wretchedly excessive consumer? The GNP counters adding the negatives to their measure of better-offness?

---

[101] World Population Data Sheet, Population Reference Bureau, Washington, D.C., 1997.

Wouldn't it be easier to just strike a balance on earth while there's still time? While we are still planning a legacy?

In making the transition to a more sustainable state, the economists need only heed their redundant mid-day maxim: "There's no such thing as a free lunch."[102] Imposing on the biodiverse web of life is not a free lunch.

GNP enthusiasts can shoulder only a portion of the blame. Our vulnerability to mass merchandisers also shares the blame.

---

[102] Garrett Hardin, *Living Within Limits*, Oxford University Press, 1993, p. 54.

22

Mass Merchandising Stimulus

It will be said, perhaps, that the increased number of purchasers in every article would give a spur to productive industry, and that the whole produce of the island would be increased. This might in some degree be the case. But the spur that these fancied riches would give to population would more than counterbalance it, and the increased produce would be to be divided among a more than proportionably increased number of people.
— Malthus, 1798, Chapter V

WHY DO WE have the massive "throughput" in this economy? What feeds this growing giant?

The economic cycle is driven by needs and wants. A need for food, clothing and shelter is a driving force. And wants are for more than subsistence.

When our needs are met, the economic flow chart is driven by wants.

Needs can be satisfied by personal choices. Wants, today, are not generally created by independent, personal choices, but rather by the manipulative schemes of merchandisers. We prefer to think of our life as a series of independent, freely motivated decisions. The sad reality is that our "freedom" becomes a mere illusion. We become defenseless servants of mass merchandisers. This vulnerability drives the unnecessary exploitation of resources.

Advertising serves an important purpose. Product information disseminated by advertisers can enable us to make informed choices. But is product information disseminated by the advertising media?

Advertisers have learned that we respond more favorably to the sale of an image than to bland information pertaining to a product. The image of a surfer skimming through a towering wave can be used to sell a car as well as a pair of slacks, although neither would be of particular benefit for the particular surfer's predicament. Scant swimsuits promote everything from cigarettes and beer to hardware and phones. Advertisers sell imagery. They no longer tell us about the products.

The advertisers' trek from product information to imagery systematically evolved during the 20th century. The year was 1920. America did not know it at the time, but one of the 200 most significant events to shape the nation was about to take place.[103] This was history in the making. Durable automobiles had, by then, essentially saturated the market. The demand for new motor vehicles was waning. The existing cars were so indestructible that many Model A and Model T Fords continue to be serviceable in South America even at the Malthusian Bicentennial. Car loans became available in 1916, but even this boost in sales was insufficient to satisfy the aspirations of General Motors. So its chairman, Alfred P. Sloan, Jr., developed a controversial marketing plan.

If the consumer no longer needed to buy a car, then there was only one way to maintain growth in the industry: get the consumer to buy something it did not need. And with that inspiration, the marketing strategy of "planned obsolescence" was presented to the American consumer. Every model year was accompanied by a faddish cosmetic alteration. Style even came at the expense of sound engineering expenditures. For example, during the gas crunch of the 1970's, American car manufacturers were still designing to meet our shallow wants, but were unable to compete with the fuel-saving engineering technology of foreign markets. Principles of planned obsolescence have prominently influenced marketing decisions. Product demand is generated by selling an image which can soon be rendered obsolete, rather than by disseminating material product information.

Mass merchandisers increasingly respond to the needs of the sellers,

---

[103] Alan Axelrod and Charles Phillips, *What Every American Should Know About American History, 200 Events that Shaped the Nation*, Bob Adams, Inc, 1992, p. 260.

not the buyers. They see us as a group of "wanna-bees." We wanna live the lifestyle promoted in the ad, no matter how tenuous this relationship might be to the product itself. No matter how sad the reality of our actual circumstance. And no matter how remote our prospect for actually living the alluring image. The purveyors of merchandise stake their claim to our allegiance by exploiting our vulnerability to this idealized image. It could be sensuality, sex, youth, athletics, thrills or dreams. Whatever your weakness, the promotional predator is close at hand. And we are easy prey.

There is perhaps no better example of our defenselessness to the wiles and stratagems of advertisers than our betrayal of human scent. A grieving spouse will often bury their head in the clothing of their deceased mate to once again relive the experience of life's natural aromas. The animal kingdom abounds with sensual messages communicated by scent. The finely tuned sensitivity of a mammal's nostrils enables sexually compelling wind-borne messages to be transmitted far and wide. Prospective mates summoned by scent from distant places allow nature's timeless sensuality and mating rituals to unfold in ecstasy season after season. Generation after generation.

There's ample precedent in the world around us to believe that our natural scents may harbor one of the most compelling forces in sexual attraction. Yet, our sense of self-doubt allowed even this measure of sexuality to be suppressed by the advertising schemes of perfumes, colognes, and cosmetics.

If our natural aroma and appearance were as repulsive as we now believe them to be, then it is astonishing that the human experiment has not rendered itself extinct by its inherent repulsiveness. Were our human ancestors the first in the fossil record to have engaged in the mating ritual in spite of, rather than because of, natural scents and images? Is the lure of advertising imagery so compelling as to corrupt us into abandoning a primeval source of sensuality?

We similarly respond to a fashion industry dictating the width of our ties and hems. We discard satisfactory articles of clothing to appease our self doubts. Clothing and other possessions become part of the waste stream to fulfill our dream of resembling a media-hyped image. But there's a sad reality for most of us. The advertised image remains a strictly hopeless quest.

This vulnerability to the purveyors of "wanna-bee" imagery is a driving force in our consumptive habits and in our destructive potential.

The most destructive blade on the economic auger spiraling into our natural resources is not driven by needs, but by wants. Our obedient response to the demands of advertisers builds speed and momentum in the auger. The windowless, faceless, bunker-like mass merchandising boxes at the distant end of glow-in-the-dark parking lots are now monuments to our dispiriting sense of self-doubt and vulnerability upon which the mass merchandisers prey.

Places nurturing a sense of place have been replaced by these new monuments. The quaint towns worthy of our respect have been abandoned for the mass merchandisers' architecturally uneventful box of consumption. It has been designed and built solely for the sake of consuming. We now shop for the sake of shopping. But our loss does not always go unnoticed. In the words of one activist: "I'd rather have a viable community than a cheap pair of underwear."[104]

Commercial messages lurk at every corner. We are besieged by 3,000 commercial messages every day.[105] Even though we do not respond to each of the advertisements, the central theme is reinforced: Buy stuff and be happy! Happiness is derived from immediate self-indulgence. Buy it now!

America was built on a tradition of duty and civic responsibility. These traditions provided an enduring bond for families and communities. A diligent work ethic enabled us to develop a grand manufacturing capability. Manufactured products eventually extended far beyond existing needs. Surpluses were created. Massive stockpiles of merchandise landed on inventory shelves. But mass-produced products would stagnate without a market. We solved the shortage of supply. Demand now needed a lift. And our shallow wants gave it

---

[104] Michael J. Sandel, *Democracy's Discontent*, Belknap Press, 1996, p. 335.

[105] Mark Landler et al, "What Happened to Advertising?" *Business Week*, September 23, 1991; Alan Durning, *How Much is Enough?*, W.W. Norton & Company, 1992.

wings.

Try this experiment at home. Mute the sound on your TV during the commercial of a nation-wide advertiser. You'll notice the scene changes every one to four seconds. Vivid imagery, rapidly exchanged scenery and bright colors are calculated to keep you riveted to the screen as long as possible. Delaying your trip to the refrigerator by even a few seconds translates into massive influence when the effect is projected over millions of viewers. Like lambs led to slaughter, we follow the not-so-subtle media message and remain indifferent to our transformation into a shopping culture.

Our susceptibility to the influence of mass merchandisers should not be underestimated. Their glitz is no match for a bunch of sentimental rubes seizing a cherished past. As burgeoning inventories accumulated, the mass merchandisers learned to capitalize on our vulnerability to immediate self-gratification. Only by rendering our possessions functionally or aesthetically obsolete, can the products of this late Industrial Revolution be foisted upon us. The apparent *happiness* in purchasing new stuff is therefore based on the media-hyped sense of *discontentment* with existing possessions. It is happiness based on discontentment. But the irony is lost on us.

Our self doubts, vulnerability to imagery and submissiveness to mass merchandisers is demonstrated by our obedient response to the advertising stimulus. We dutifully learn to shop. Shop. And Shop till we drop. Shop for the sake of shopping. Shop. Our faith, hope and destiny. As though picking up another plastic lawn chair from the tabloid strewn check-out counter at the lamentable box looming at the end of a parking lagoon will somehow save us from ourselves.

Aesthetics and a sense of civic pride no longer hamper our subservient response. Mesmerized by the lure of a mega-mall's commercial messages, we are unable to distinguish our civic responsibilities from shopping. Economic growth, after all, requires us to be good consumers. Our lives are now governed less by what we believe than by how we consume.

Our shopping edifices are no longer built for the ages. While we enjoy unparalleled prosperity, we build dismal and sprawling structures with a design-life corresponding to the term of the mortgage. Our auto dependent, low-density, segregated housing opportunities are no longer worthy of our enduring respect. In the words of James Howard Kunstler:

> The road is now like television, violent and tawdry. The landscape it runs through is littered with cartoon buildings and commercial messages. We whiz by them at fifty-five miles an hour and forget them, because one convenience store looks like the next. They do not celebrate anything beyond their mechanistic ability to sell merchandise. We don't want to remember them. We did not savor the approach and we were not rewarded upon reaching the destination, and it will be the same next time, and every time. There is little sense of having arrived anywhere, because every place looks like no place in particular.[106]

Have we been reduced to mere pawns on somebody else's economic chessboard? Has civic duty suffered the same indignity as natural havens now engulfed by landfills? Can we no longer find a meaningful existence beyond the realm of excessive consumption? Can voluntary simplicity still lead to a fulfilling lifestyle? Are we so enchanted by the lure of an image, a dream and a lifestyle, that we can't see the mighty flow of merchandise in our "throughput?" Can we no longer sense the acceleration of this destructive potential? Will our indifference to limits ceaselessly blind us to the risks of "perpetual" economic growth? Will our measure of success forever be based on consumption rather than conviction?

---

[106] James Howard Kunstler, *The Geography of Nowhere*, Simon & Schuster, 1993, p. 131.

Part Four

GROWTH ON THE LAND

23

CONQUEST AND DISCOVERY

A wider and more extensive territory was successively occupied. A broader desolation extended all around them. Want pinched the less fortunate members of the society; and, at length, the impossibility of supporting such a number together became too evident to be resisted. Young scions were then pushed out from the parent-stock and instructed to explore fresh regions and to gain happier seats for themselves by their swords. 'The world was all before them where to choose.' Restless from present distress, flushed with the hope of fairer prospects, and animated with the spirit of hardy enterprise, these daring adventurers were likely to become formidable adversaries to all who opposed them. The peaceful inhabitants of the countries on which they rushed could not long withstand the energy of men acting under such powerful motives of exertion.

— Malthus, 1798, Chapter III

IN SOME CASES growth is a good. But if you're an oncologist, it's not.

Human indifference to limits is now found in atmospheric heights and on ocean depths. But its most visible and graphic display is now indelibly etched on the landscape.

According to the American Farmland Trust, 1.1 million acres of prime crop land are devoured by urban sprawl on the American landscape every year.[107] This amounts to over 3,000 acres of farmland per day. It is 126 acres per hour. And over two acres per minute in the United States! We tend to think of the colonists as the colonizers of

---

[107] Keith Schneider and Florence Schneider, "America's Farthest-Reaching Environmental Issue," *Great Lakes Bulletin*, Winter, 1997, p. 6.

land. Our rate of land colonization make the colonists look like Johnnie Appleseed on a Sunday picnic. They are tame by comparison to the present-day level of colonization.

The aggressive loss of farmland coincides with the World Watch Institute's report that we have crossed the worldwide threshold of *per capita* food production. The food quantity available for each person is now shrinking. Population increases assure this trend will continue.[108] As of the Malthusian bicentennial we are adding almost 100 million additional people to the breakfast nook every year. Food production is not keeping pace. But we are still busily paving farms for the sake of growth.

According to the American Farmland Trust, between 1970 and 1990, the Chicago area population increased by only 4%. Land consumption, however, increased by an astonishing 46% during the same period. Before World War II we built five homes to the acre, on average. Today's newly built residence displaces over one acre of land. It also furthers the abandonment of properties in our urban core.[109]

The State of Michigan loses 10 acres of agricultural land per hour, 24 hours of every day.[110] This is not confined to a mere 8-hour work shift. This statistic continues round-the-clock even on weekends and holidays. Michigan's conversion of farmland results in an annual loss of approximately $100 million in local farm revenue.[111]

The aggressive modifications to a valued agricultural heritage cannot continue for even the lifetimes of our children. Nevertheless, the pace

---

[108] Lester R. Brown and Hal Kane, *Full House*, W.W. Norton & Company, 1994.

[109] Comments of Mark Wyckoff, editor of *Michigan Planning and Zoning News* at a Town Meeting at North Central Michigan College in Petoskey, Michigan on November 25, 1996.

[110] Michigan Society of Planning Officials, *PATTERNS ON THE LAND: Our Choices— Our Future*, September, 1995, p. 24.

[111] Id, p. 24.

of farmland conversion[112] continues unabated. While the planet is busy increasing the need for agricultural products, we are still busy eliminating agricultural lands.

By what right do we claim this ability to compromise the nutritional interests of our successors? How do we justify this massive loss of farmland? Where did this begin? History can be our guide in making sense of claims to the land.

Land has historically been claimed by a right of conquest. Might was right long before the Peloponnesian Wars were fought. Surely, even before recorded history.

Does the American claim to land arise out of conquest?

Not according to the U.S. Supreme Court in the early 19th century.

Where do the notions of property rights trace their origin? The legal claim to land in America stems from a claim of discovery, according to the U.S. Supreme Court. Columbus is said to have "discovered" America (notwithstanding the presence of a Native American civilization). This notion of "discovery" became more than a metaphor. It has ascended to a prominent legal principle.

In 1823, the U.S. Supreme Court was called upon to determine the rightful owner of land. On the one hand, the Plaintiff claimed title through Native American ownership. The Defendant claimed title by virtue of the Europeans' "discovery" of the land. In this case,[113] the U.S. Supreme Court stated:

> Discovery is the foundation of title in European nations, and this overlooks all proprietary rights in the natives . . .

> On the discovery of this immense continent, the great nations of Europe were eager to appropriate to themselves so much of it as they could respectively acquire. Its vast extent offered an ample field to the ambition and enterprise of all . . .

---

[112] "Development" is a term deliberately avoided.

[113] *Johnson v M'intosh*, 8 Wheat 543; 5 L Ed 681 (1823). The Defendant's name is generally pronounced "McIntosh" notwithstanding the inconsistent spelling.

Spain did not rest her title solely on the grant of the Pope. Her discussions respecting boundary, with France, with Great Britain, and with the United States, all show that she placed it on the rights given by discovery. Portugal sustained her claim to the Brazils by the same title.

France, also, founded her title to the vast territories she claimed in America on discovery . . .

However extravagant the pretension of converting the discovery of an inhabited country into conquest may appear, if the principle has been asserted in the first instance, and afterwards sustained; if a country has been acquired and held under it; if the property of the great mass of the community originates in it, it becomes the law of the land, and cannot be questioned. So, too, with respect to the concomitant principle, that the Indian inhabitants are to be considered merely as occupants, to be protected, indeed, while in peace, in the possession of their lands, but to be deemed incapable of transferring the absolute title to others.

The illusion of unlimited frontiers ("this immense continent") and "discovery" influenced the 1823 U.S. Supreme Court. It became the law of the land. Does this view seem dated? Out-moded? Obsolete? Well, it probably is. Yet it may still influence our conception of property.

The euphoric "finders-keepers" mentality of yesterday's colonists and the 1823 Supreme Court seems to have morphed into a "buyers-keepers" mentality today. Farmers unable to pay high property taxes surrender to the so-called "developers" waiting in the wings to "discover" a new economic opportunity. To cash out a valued agricultural heritage. To terminate a family legacy. To eliminate a rich rural - urban cultural mix with the adjoining community.

"Development" of the land entombs nature's pulsations with asphalt, the final cash crop. In a fit of arrogance, they name the "development" after what was left behind. Titles now herald casualties in the wake of their "progress." Accordingly, signs litter the highway with new subdivisions along "Farm Lane." Gone is the farm and with it went the culture of agrarian values. New roads now lead to "Eagle's Nest Apartments," and "Deer Run Condominium." Anyone spot an eagle or deer there lately?

According to the 1823 U.S. Supreme Court, the right to own land emanates not so much from bloodshed and conquest, but rather from "discovery." Under our more civilized standards, we now euphemistically rely upon options, margins, points, origination fees, commissions, mergers, LBOs and acquisitions. From the vantage of the economic opportunist, it is still a matter of discovering a money making plan. But from the vantage of the family farmer's shattered dreams, the view may be akin to that of the Native American whose land was "discovered" by European settlers. It might still be a matter of conquest. Not by brutal bloodshed, but today by financial fiat.

Paradoxically, we pave unspoiled land to generate enough money to escape to natural havens now and then. Like an overplayed TV rerun, we replay this skit endlessly, *ad nauseum*. Shuffle money to degrade a farm or forest and then shuffle ourselves to a natural retreat from the madness. But relief is only temporary. More "progress" is sure to follow. Is there still enough unpaved land for this rerun to keep replaying itself for the lifetime of our children?

When we ponder why America is losing over 2 acres of productive agricultural land every minute in a land-consumptive frenzy, our infatuation with lawns can't be overlooked. Why have we expanded the average lot size from one-fifth of an acre to over one acre? Why have we introduced vast distances between people? Why have we rendered ourselves utterly dependent on cars and therefore the depletion of fossil fuels?

Is our love of the lawn a possible contributing cause?

Americans own ten times more lawnmowers, *per capita*, than the rest of the world. Perhaps, if we could just suppress our affinity for monotony in nature (a monocultural lawn with banished insects, the pollinating invaders), then maybe we could more meaningfully appreciate our place entwined in nature's web of life. And we could start building our homes on smaller, less land-consumptive lots.

In the mid-1970s, there was a semi-serious proposal on how to control urban sprawl. Rather than challenge the property rights advocates in zoning battles, they proposed simply banning lawnmowers.[114] Maybe there's something to this.

Shakespeare said: "All the world's a stage." As our drama unfolds, we actively inflict harm, and we passively become spectators· in the systematic dismantling of nature's biodiverse heritage. We lack an appreciation for the lost diversity in nature. We become an active participant in bringing our non-human companions to the brink of extinction. The forgotten pollinators no longer have a reason to visit our created habitats. Do we urbanize 2 acres of U.S. farmland per minute for this? To actively suppress nature's wonders in favor of an unimaginative monocultural grass?

Our hefty appetite for land often stems from our allegiance to "growth." We faithfully cling to the unexamined conviction that perpetual growth on a finite planet is not only possible, but also desirable. We consider growth to inevitably be seen as a positive development. Yet this form of growth is, in reality, stagnation. An advanced form of imaginative stagnation. It is the mindless repetition of land use casualties across the nation.

The all-consumptive affinity for growth has also been characterized as a form of addiction. It comes complete with states of denial, trauma recovery, suffering and co-dependency.[115]

The so-called "pro-growthers" profess "You can't stop progress." O.K. But what can we do to arrest mental stagnation? And how shall we control an addiction?

Here is another aspect of our character: competition.

---

[114] Comments of Mark Wyckoff, Editor of *Michigan Planning and Zoning News*, at a Town Meeting at North Central Michigan College on November 25, 1996.

[115] Chellis Glendinning, *My Name is Chellis and I'm in Recovery from Western Civilization*, Shambhala, 1994.

24

CIVILITY AND COMPETITION

The scarcity of farms is a very general complaint in England. And the competition in every kind of business is so great that it is not possible that all should be successful.
— Malthus, 1798, Chapter IV

W E "GROW" SUBDIVISIONS on farmland. This is called "growth." We look for our stocks to "grow." Economic "growth" is considered good. Yet, we can have too much of a good thing. Ice cream is good, but ingesting too much ice cream will cause us to confront limits. Physical limits. Similarly, nothing but "growth" compels us to confront limits. We cannot remain indifferent. We are in denial at our peril.

Ponder the root cause of "growth." Is it our need to acquire stuff? Our acquisitiveness? Does competition become a factor in growth? How might civility influence growth?

We strive to nurture friendships. We are taught to treat others with dignity and respect, and we long for similar treatment. Civility finds a comfortable dwelling place in our hearts.

Yet, beneath the veil of civility lies the harsh reality that life is a team sport and the world remains a competitive place. Our basic sustenance is a product of competition. It has always been a matter of whether our team can out-compete theirs. Only the "ours" and the "theirs" change.

We cannot eat a hamburger or don a pair of leather shoes without terminating the life of a cow. Well, OK, the cow went placidly. But no one stopped to ask how she felt about longevity.

Sometimes the world is just not a friendly place. Even nice folk sometimes turn a cold shoulder. From a chicken's perspective, egg farmers and consumers are a conspiracy of thieves.

After writing a shelf full of books on *The Story of Civilization*, the authors attempted to compress thirty to forty centuries of script into a 100 page text entitled *The Lessons of History*.[116] In this book the authors reflect on the role of competition in our world:

> So the first biological lesson of history is that life is competition. Competition is not only the life of trade, it is the trade of life - peaceful when food abounds, violent when the mouths outrun the food. Animals eat one another without qualm; civilized men consume one another by due process of law. Co-operation is real, and increases with social development, but mostly because it is a tool and form of competition; we co-operate in our group - our family, community, club, church, party, "race," or nation - in order to strengthen our group in its competition with other groups. Competing groups have the qualities of competing individuals; acquisitiveness, pugnacity, partisanship, pride.

One person's wealth is defined by another's deprivation. Ten chickens and two goats may represent monumental wealth in some circles. In others, wealth is defined by the number of cars, jet skis, snow mobiles, four-wheelers and by an obscene ability to contribute to the atmospheric and terrestrial waste stream. Wealth is a relative commodity. It is often a product of competition.

Competition among people defines our place. This is how it works in the Olympics as well as in the stock market. Competition is not only an attribute of humanity, but also essential to survival. Competition with the surrounding forms of plant and animal life maintains our existence.

But we are not the only competitors. With the exception of plants capable of photosynthesizing sunlight into energy, every member of the food chain maintains itself by extinguishing another form of animal or vegetable life. And even the plants are vigorous competitors over the

---

[116] Will and Ariel Durant, *The Lessons of History*, MJF Books, published in arrangement with Simon & Schuster, Inc, 1968, p. 19.

scarce resource of the day: light, water or nutrients. Competition prevails for sharks and lions, and also for microscopic forms of life and minuscule invertebrates. It is even true for herbivores. They survive only by extinguishing plant life.

A world of cooperation, competition, treachery and deception unfolds daily in your local wood lot. A descent into the universe of ants and invertebrates will disclose not only a caring nurturing society, but also a brutal animal kingdom predisposed to violence.[117]

Perhaps the vegetarians of the world believe they live above rules of conquest. But it is a fantasy. To enjoy a tomato, they must first sever it from its life-giving vine. Then, to derive nourishment, they draw the last vestige of life from the tomato's body and infuse it into their own. Even an underground potato must first suffer a fatal blow before sustaining the vegetarian.

Impeccable lawns are maintained only through the introduction of deadly pesticides and herbicides. The onslaught of uninvited insects and unwanted "weeds" continues unabated. The only issue is whether our team's scientific muscle can stem the tide and save the monocultural clear-cut lawn. All the while, our non-human companions tirelessly compete for their place in the sun or for their niche in nature.

On the front lawn it's us versus them. But even away from our lawns, competition reigns supreme. The majestic drama unfolds as we placidly walk among the towering pines. Nature's beauty may camouflage the bitter tenacity with which its participants cling to their niche and defend their turf. Beneath the veil of intense beauty resides a world of intense competition. This was recognized in even the title to Darwin's 1859 book: *The Origin of Species by Means of Natural Selection, or, The Preservation of Favored Races in the Struggle for Life.*

As Malthus observed, competition becomes particularly harsh in the face of scarcity. This is the "vice" component of his "misery and vice." Experiments reveal rats can peacefully coexist when they are in balance with their surroundings. But when they overpopulate a room and exceed the carrying capacity of their existing environment, they turn on each other. A room teeming with overflowing rats will graphically

---

[117] Bert Holldobler and Edward O. Wilson, *Journey to the Ants*, Belknap Press, 1994.

depict the vice of nature's harsh competitive reality in the face of scarcity. They will attack each other with cannibalistic intent.[118] Similarly, gangs of our close cousins, the chimpanzees, wage brutal border wars to protect their lands.[119] The frequency and intensity of aggression and violence increases with the density of lower primates.[120]

Stephen Jay Gould has used a similar principle to explain the unlikelihood of finding advanced civilizations in far reaches of the universe:

> Perhaps any society that could build a technology for such interplanetary, if not intergalactic, travel must first pass through a period of potential destruction where technological capacity outstrips social or moral restraint. And perhaps no, or very few, societies can ever emerge intact from such a crucial episode.[121]

The civility we enjoy results in part from the good fortune in stumbling upon seemingly abundant resources and harvests. Vast minerals, deep rich soils, clear waters and abundant forests helplessly awaited exploitation when the land was "discovered." We have learned to successfully manipulate the surroundings. Civility fares well for the victors in a bountiful habitat. But will it remain bountiful? Will unlimited population and economic growth eventually press up against limits? How well is civility upheld in places of shortages, such as Somalia, Rwanda and Bosnia?

Our brief encounters with scarcity did not bode well for the human prospect. Resource wars in the Persian Gulf were carried on at a safe distance. Thousands of lost Iraqi lives soon became forgotten electronic impulses on our remote TV monitors. It is difficult to

---

[118] Konrad Lorenz, *King Solomon's Ring*, Mentor, 1952, p. 37.

[119] Jeffrey Kluger, "Females in Charge," *Time Magazine*, Oct. 14, 1996, p. 80.

[120] Frans de Waal, *Good Natured*, Harvard University Press, 1996.

[121] Stephen Jay Gould, *Full House*, Harmony Books, 1996.

vicariously appreciate the drama of a resource war while venturing into the battlefield on TV land armed with nothing more than a remote control. Channel surfing provides quick relief. Forgetfulness is now the way we happily cope with our skirmish with scarcity.

Efforts to eliminate competition and aggression are unrealistic. In the interest of maintaining civility in social affairs, we might well contemplate how to avoid bouts with scarcity and how to establish satisfactory rules for controlling aggression in the future. This will lead to a better prospect for civility than if we perpetuate the illusion that life is not a team sport, the world is a cooperative place, not competitive, and there will always be bountiful harvests no matter how many of us show up for dinner.

Competition can cause the world to become an ugly place. The issue is not whether civility will triumph over brutality. Rather, the defining challenge requires us to establish a coherent pattern for civility and competition to peacefully co-exist.

Our species is capable of a variety of responses to scarcity. Competition is one alternative. Cooperation and civility is another. The decision to select cooperation just becomes more difficult in the face of scarcity.

We will minimize the risk of aggressive and violent competition if we learn to diminish the prospect for scarcity. This requires us to define our place in the scheme of things. To define a balance with the web of life from which we have emerged. To see ourselves as a subsystem within a larger ecosystem. To limit our fertility and control migration before population excesses claim unsuspecting victims. To avert the prospect of the "Malthusian crunch." To define a sustainable balance for ourselves and our successors.

Learning to manage competition is more realistic than hoping to eliminate it. In his classic account of animal behavior, Konrad Z. Lorenz observes how wolves have evolved social inhibitions in tandem with the development of their fearsome teeth. In wolves' male dominance rituals, a submissive loser will expose his throat to the victor. Lethal teeth will gesture toward the neck, but will not clamp down. Hierarchy is thereby established, harm is averted and the wolf pack remains united. Lorenz then explains the risk of hazardous man-made technology developing faster than our social skills:

> When, in the course of its evolution, a species of animals develops a weapon which may destroy a fellow-member at one blow, then, in order to survive, it must develop, along with the weapon, a social inhibition to prevent a usage which could endanger the existence of the species . . . We did not receive our weapons from nature. We made them ourselves, of our own free will. Which is going to be easier for us in the future, the production of weapons or the engendering of the feeling of responsibility that should go along with them, the inhibitions without which our race must perish by virtue of its own creations? We must build up these inhibitions purposefully for we cannot rely on our instincts.[122]

Our competitive nature is exhibited in stock market ticker tapes and investment growth portfolios. Whether intended or unintended, the effects result in scars on the landscape. Purposeful inhibitions and a workable set of rules await our attention on the frontiers of competition, growth, economics and fertility.

We may also consider inhibiting our affinity for the vehicle of escape now driving consumptive land use decisions. Perhaps there's nothing much wrong with America that a good gas crunch or a hefty gas tax couldn't fix.

---

[122] Lorenz, Konrad Z., *King Solomon's Ring*, Mentor, New York, 1952, pp. 209-211.

25

DRIVEN TO EXTREMES

In the natural progress of a state towards riches, manufactures and foreign commerce would follow, in their order, the high cultivation of the soil. — Malthus, 1798, Chapter XVII

T HE INDIFFERENCE TO limits perversely compromises not only the future, but also the present. Perhaps it results from an inability to perceive limits. Maybe it stems from an unwillingness to acknowledge the existence of limits. It influences how we plan the civic equipment for our cities. It affects how we view our communities and even how we relate to each other. Land use planning determines how we live our lives. But what determines land use planning? Since World War II, our communities have no longer been designed around a town commons, a central focal point or around healthy exchanges among diverse community members. Rather, community planning has been fashioned by an indifference to limits.

This indifference finds expression in our frenzied lust for the motor vehicle. We pull up to the gas pump as though the other end is connected to an unlimited supply. As though the geological dipstick on fossil fuel reserves will perpetually register "full." Conspicuously charmless urban designs for motorcar transport now render historic towns and their occupants economic casualties. The once thriving central business district brought the community together. This is where we came to maintain a sense of accountability and responsibility to each other. It has now been replaced by land consumptive urban sprawl which nurtures anonymity and leads to the abandonment of our historic places. Abandoned buildings and abandoned people now fill the void.

Malthus would likely note the rapid colonization of agricultural land and open space.[123] Were he writing on root causes of the indifference to limits of urban growth, he would inescapably focus on the automobile and its graceless influence on land use planning. In the words of Henry David Thoreau: "There are a thousand hacking at the branches of evil to one who is striking at the root."[124]

Enchanted by the glow of a new chrome grill, we become desensitized to its harsh gaze. Swept by the surge of acceleration, we obligingly accommodate pollutants and CO_2 emissions. The car persists as the American dream, yet its influence has a nightmarish quality.

Can the 1.3 billion people in China's economy, each with individual priorities and needs, move from bicycles to motor vehicles without dramatically influencing the price or supply of fossil fuels? Can the world become a safer place by exchanging massive wealth and massive weaponry for Middle Eastern fossil fuels? Will the millions faithfully surrendering their lives to a religious Jihad to earn the respect of their Maker be in a position to exercise responsible restraint with these weapons?

Our admiration of the motorcar has changed the face of America. At one time, our communities nurtured a sense of community. They were like living organisms allowing a healthy mix of people of all ages and abilities. Everyone had access to the amenities of the village.[125]

Today's children no longer have meaningful access to the civic equipment in a community. The civic equipment includes the public places, recreational areas, coffee shops and gathering places. Who

---

[123] Michigan Society of Planning Officials, *PATTERNS ON THE LAND: Our Choices— Our Future*, September, 1995.

[124] Henry David Thoreau, *Walden*, 1854.

[125] Peter Katz, *The New Urbanism*, Mc-Graw-Hill, Inc., 1994; Constance E. Beaumont, *How Superstore Sprawl Can Harm Communities*, National Trust for Historic Preservation, 1994; James Howard Kunstler, *The Geography of Nowhere*, Simon & Schuster, Inc., 1994; James Howard Kunstler, *Home From Nowhere*, Simon & Schuster, Inc., 1996; Thomas Hylton, *Save Our Land Save Our Towns*, RB Books, 1995; David Engwicht, *Reclaiming Our Cities & Towns*, New Society Publishers, 1993.

would set their child loose in a mega-mall parking lot? We no longer plan our towns around a shared sense of place. Happy people have been replaced with happy cars.

In peering at our created habitat we catch a glimpse of ourselves. Our lives. Towns now betray a dispiriting design. Isolated subdivisions segregate us by age, wealth, class and status. We'll whiz by the created habitat as we cocoon in our cars with swivel cups, cellular phones, fax machines, CDs and climate control. We become so dispossessed of our natural surroundings that even the artificial lemon fragrance injected by the car wash attendant seems a natural amenity of this private realm.

Our community planners have been reduced to indentured servants of highway engineers. Are they really planning a community? They label themselves "community planners." But while planning roads for our swift flight, do they pause to consider why we find it necessary to flee? Why are "community planners" no longer planning the elements of a "community"?

With every new insight into their zoning ordinances, the community planners become more adept at plying their craft. Their analysis, even their vernacular, tends to converge on a common norm. They talk the planners' talk. They walk the planners' walk. This is at once their strength and their weakness. Appreciation of the intricacies in a zoning ordinance is acquired only over time. Each passing issue hones their skills. Eventually every nook and cranny in the zoning ordinance is ground on the wheels of justice. They become more fluent with finite zoning laws, and yet with each new insight into the law, they shed another level of perception of the big picture.

Distances beyond a pedestrian limit are introduced between all civic activities. Soccer moms become modern-day cab drivers. Work, play, school, institutions, town halls, parks and civic functions are all carried out at remotely zoned locations. Motor vehicle licensure becomes a form of citizenship. Banished are the frail and elderly. Ostracized are the children. And compromised is our sense of community.

Traditional towns are abandoned in favor of unabashed ugliness. This replicates itself on suburban farms as we homogenize the face of America. It is the architecturally disappointing box hovering at the distant edge of an asphalt parking lot. It is accessed only by car.

Turning a child loose in the urban setting with a bicycle is now a form of child abuse.

Motor vehicle mania has taken a compelling hold of our collective conscience. We are benumbed to the surroundings. We perceive ourselves to be in the driver's seat, yet we have become the driven.

Endangered historic structures and architectural monuments of our forebears still represent a tribute to traditional community pride. They were built for the ages. Constructed with handcrafted pride and tools passed from generation to generation as a family legacy, they remain a tribute to the cherished carless past. But even these pillars of history have become abandoned tombstones across America.

Civic duty now suffers the same indignity as urban patterns of the earlier era. Abandoned places, boarded store fronts and America's underprivileged now form the void left by the car crazed. And we are only beginning to pay the social carrying costs of this abandonment.

Gone are multiple use zones and centralized transit systems. Gone are places worthy of our enduring commitment. Gone are sidewalks and front porches, because no one is walking by anyway. Gone are communities. In is consumerism. In is consumption. And in are cars.

As an abiding gravestone to our affinity for the motor vehicle, abandoned car parts now even litter some urban lawns. Marauding eyesores sap the pride of a community.

So it breeds more gruesome ugliness. So we're dependent on our car for every move we make. So we are rendering ourselves utterly dependent on fossil fuels. So we're vulnerable to any instability in the price or supply of fossil fuels. So the driver's license has become a symbol of citizenship. So a single mother seldom encounters the traditional American family due to her segregation by zoning. So Grandma is ushered into her "adult community" and everyone else is driven out. So children are deprived of inter-generational experiences in their daily lives. So the embellishments found in traditional architecture are now replaced by strip malls. So we no longer notice the unsightliness of parking lagoons with bunker-type structures. So we are indifferent to the limits of fossil fuel reserves. Does it matter? Has the car driven us from the heart and soul of America?

The indifference to limits in fossil fuel consumption is now the driving force in how we plan our communities and therefore how we live our lives. Towns were at one time planned around central public transit. Instability in the price or supply of petroleum will eventually again relegate us to public transit. The vulnerability of sprawling urban designs may then become apparent.

There are limits to our ability to deplete resources. To pave farms. To abandon history. To ignore community. To distance ourselves from the civic realm. We can rise above the frontier's romantic mystique while there's still time. Regrettably, views on "property rights" formed during the frontier era rise as obstacles to responsible planning and a recognition of limits. Historic views on "property rights" nurture the persistent illusion of endless purple mountains' majesty and boundless amber waves of grain.

26

PROPERTY RIGHTS

The advocate for the present order of things is apt to treat the sect of speculative philosophers either as a set of artful and designing knaves, who preach up ardent benevolence and draw captivating pictures of a happier state of society, only the better to enable them to destroy the present establishments and to forward their own deep-laid schemes of ambitions; or as wild and mad-headed enthusiasts, whose silly speculations and absurd paradoxes are not worthy the attention of any reasonable man.
— Malthus, 1798, Chapter I

ENVIRONMENTAL REGULATIONS RESTRICT human activity on land. This can cut into a property owner's sense of freedom and hoped-for economic gain. A backlash to the environmental movement has been formed. It hoists a "property rights" banner and it has been labeled the "brownlash movement."[126]

In common parlance, the words "property rights" are oxymoronic. The phrase has more to do with "perceived people rights" than with rights of the property. The phrase can be used to justify "property wrongs." We do not use the phrase "property wrongs" or "perceived people rights," but rather, "property rights."

With a flair for conformity, the words "property rights" will reluctantly be used in their common parlance. This phrase often refers to a person's legal right to abuse the land. These rights are claimed to arise out of property ownership.

---

[126] Paul R. Ehrlich and Anne H. Ehrlich, *Betrayal of Science and Reason*, Island Press, 1996.

Property rights in an organized society have never been unlimited. In feudal times, property interests were not transferable and were entirely subject to the King's whim.

After feudal times, property rights were expanded, but not without limit. Ownership interests remain subject to forfeiture upon non-payment of taxes. Even the right to leave property to one's heirs is limited by governmental regulations regarding spousal rights, liens for debts, and formal rules in drafting a will.[127]

Our perception of property rights can be influenced by our perception of scarcity. There's no need to conserve on an asset in unlimited supply. No one practices good husbandry with respect to mosquitoes on a mid-summer night.

The classic illustration distinguishing scarcity from abundance involves the relative value of diamonds and water. This economic value depends chiefly on how thirsty you are.[128]

Dwindling frontiers and a depth of knowledge influence our perception of harm. As our forebears peered looked to the west, they saw a land of endless horizons and unlimited resources. These perceptions may have influenced John Locke to make the following observations about property rights in 1690:

> Nor was this appropriation of any parcel of land, by improving it, any prejudice to any other man, since there was still enough and as good left; and more than the yet unprovided could use. So that in effect there was never the less left for others because of his enclosure for himself. For he that leaves as much as another can make use of, does as good as take nothing at all. Nobody could think himself injured by the drinking of another man, though he took a good draught, who had a whole river of the same water left

---

[127] James L. McElfish, Jr., Philip Warburg, John Pendergrass, *Property: Past, Present, Future*, Environmental Law Institute, Research Brief No. 6, October, 1996.

[128] Tom Bailey, Reflections, *Update*, quarterly conservation newsletter of the Little Traverse Conservancy, Volume XVII, No. 4, Winter, 1996.

him to quench his thirst; and the case of land and water, where there is enough of both, is perfectly the same.[129]

Mr. Locke's observations of the American frontier preceded the era of flammable rivers and toxic aquatic life.

On July 12, 1893, Frederick Jackson Turner, an obscure history professor from the University of Wisconsin, spoke at the World Columbian Exposition at the Art Institute in Chicago. His view of resources differed from Locke's. Turner foreshadowed the future environmentalists' sensitivity to limits. Taking note of the 1890 census, Mr. Turner recognized the end of the American frontier. Land was, by then, claimed under a right of ownership from sea to shining sea. By announcing the end of this colorful chapter in American history, Mr. Turner dramatically influenced the way we see ourselves and our past.[130]

Our analysis of harm largely depends on whether we still see the world with Lockean optimism. Do we still envision ourselves to be peering over the Alleghenies? Can we again summon Turner's foresight to develop a sense for limits?

Perhaps no harm resulted when our first swamp was drained and the first landfill was created. No harm befalls the ecosystem by swatting a fly. As Locke stated above: "For he that leaves as much as another can make use of, does as good as take nothing at all."

It is not a question of whether we will start to perceive harm resulting from current activities. We already have. It is only a question of when the daunting prospects so squarely confront us that we can no longer postpone a remedy. We can only temporarily dodge the issue. Escape is an illusion, not a choice.

Even John Locke, the water resource optimist in colonial times,

---

[129] Locke, John, *Treatise of Civil Government and a Letter Concerning Toleration*, Irvington Publishers, Inc., N.Y., Chapter V, of Property.

[130] Professor Turner's historic speech of 1893 has been identified as one of "200 Events that Shaped the Nation" in *What Every American Should Know About History*, by Axelrod and Phillips, Bob Adams, Inc. Publishers, 1992. The full text of Professor Turner's speech is published by the *Social Contract*, Social Contract Press, January, 1994.

recognized the need for regulation in a social compact:

> For it would be a direct contradiction for any one to enter into society with others for the securing and regulating of property, and yet to suppose his land . . . should be exempt from the jurisdiction of that government to which he himself, and the property of the land, is a subject.[131]

John Locke also stated:

> . . . the great and chief end . . . of men's uniting into commonwealths, and putting themselves under the government, is the preservation of their property.[132]

Benjamin Franklin similarly recognized a person's right to property depended upon the existence of a society:

> Private property therefore is a creature of society, and is subject to the calls of that society, whenever its necessities shall require it, even to its last farthing; its contributions therefore to the public exigencies are not to be considered as conferring a benefit on the public, entitling the contributors to the distinctions of honor and power, but as a return of an obligation previously received or the payment of a just debt.[133]

As our horizons dwindle, and as we develop the scientific tools to assess our impact to the world around us, we are increasingly caused to reevaluate the scope of property rights. The well-being of our successors will depend on how we respond to advancing scarcity.

---

[131] Locke, John, *Two Treatises of Government Book II*, Section 120.

[132] James M. McElfish, Jr., Philip Warburg, John Pendergrass, "Property: Past, Present, Future," Environmental Law Institute, Research Brief No. 6, October, 1996, p. 4.

[133] Id, at p. 5.

There is scarcity in the absorptive capacity of environmental sinks (atmosphere and landfills), in the resilience of biodiversity, in the malleability of natural habitats, in the protective ozone shield's ability to withstand chemical invasion, and in the number of not-next-door places for future landfills. At one time we were advancing on the frontier. But now the frontier is advancing on us. It arrives in the form of toxic air, degraded groundwaters and depleted non-renewable resources. Will we respond to scarcity by placing a paramount value on the rights of a property owner to further diminish scarce resources? Or will "property rights" place a value on the rights of the property? Will we grant legal standing to the land upon which we rely and upon our successors whose interests are being compromised?

When the need for regulation bumps up against a property owner's profit motives, we find compassion and foresight confronting greed, boundless optimism and an indifference to limits. Short-term economic interests often prevail. The resulting battle hasn't yet taken to the streets, but it rages on a constitutional terrain under the heading of "takings law." This is now where judicial indifference to limits can come to full bloom. A number of formidable conservation battles will continue to be fought over the takings issue.

27

TAKINGS LAW

Among plants and animals the view of the subject is simple. They are all impelled by a powerful instinct to the increase of their species, and this instinct is interrupted by no reasoning, or doubts about providing for their offspring. Wherever therefore there is liberty, the power of increase is exerted; and the superabundant effects are repressed afterwards by want of room and nourishment, which is common to animals and plants; and among animals, by becoming the prey of others.

The effects of this check on man are more complicated.
— Malthus, 1798, Chapter II

So-CALLED "TAKINGS LAW" arises out of twelve words in the Fifth Amendment to the U.S. Constitution: "nor shall private property be taken for public use, without just compensation." We are not likely to dispel the mystique of the Fifth Amendment on the Malthusian bicentennial, but we might develop an appreciation for its operation on a fragile landscape.

When the government "takes" your home for a public highway, no one will question your right to compensation. You have suffered a Fifth Amendment "taking" of private property. The land has truly been "taken" from your possession.

But what if the government does not physically invade your land? What if it dents your economic value with an environmental regulation? The law might prohibit desecration of a wetland. Perhaps it restricts construction on a fragile dune. Maybe it keeps you from erecting a garage on the tenuous nesting site of an endangered species. This field of law is indexed under "Regulatory Takings." In other words,

Regulatory Takings laws apply when property value is not impaired by the government's physical invasion of the land, but rather by a regulation, such as an environmental or zoning law. The government has not physically "taken" your land, it has only "taken" value by a regulation. Ergo, Regulatory Taking.

As a practical matter, every regulation of land could affect value in some way. Every tree ordinance, zoning law or community health standard could, in some way, impair a person's property value.

Some environmental regulations meet everyone's approval. No compensation is due for complying with these regulations. Nuclear waste, for example, cannot be dumped in your residential backyard. Your backyard might be worth millions if you could sell it as a nuclear waste site. But the inability to strike it rich by disposing of radioactive material in your backyard just doesn't give rise to a compensable Fifth Amendment "taking." No one seriously submits an invoice to Uncle Sam for complying with this law.

The field of Regulatory Takings balances individual rights against social responsibilities. The principle of law remains stable, but its application to particular facts fluctuates according to our perceptions of harm. Conduct permissible in an unpopulated land of vast resources may not be tolerated in a dense urban center. One person's freedom to swing their fist stops at the tip of another person's nose.

The law of Regulatory Takings is of particular interest in a free and democratic union. Maximizing freedom became the defining challenge for the framers of our Constitution. The absence of any rules, or anarchy, might create a temporary illusion of freedom. But the experiment will likely be cut short when the first trespasser pierces the sanctity of another's home and there's no where to turn for help. On the other end of the spectrum, pervasive and rigid laws constrict the right to life, liberty and the pursuit of happiness. Such laws stifle our ingenuity and do not advance the cause of freedom. It becomes a matter of balance.

The constitutional framers tried to establish a framework of rules within which freedom could flourish. They tried to strike a meaningful balance between these seemingly conflicting properties (rules vs. freedom). And we are still met with the same challenge under the Fifth

Amendment in Regulatory Takings.

The law of Regulatory Takings prompts consideration of the circumstances in a free and democratic union in which responsibility to others trumps a person's right to do as they please with their property. When does civic duty upstage property rights? And when can mutual responsibility be left to fend for itself? If consideration of future generations becomes a matter of voluntary participation, then will standards be set by the least considerate among us? Will the principles of decency in land use now be set by whoever is willing to stoop to the lowest depth of depravity?

Some claim Regulatory Takings law requires public funds be paid to us for acting as good stewards of the future. They see it as a conservation ethic at the taxpayer's expense. A clean conscience purchased with public dole. As though a heart and soul for tomorrow's children can be bought with cold cash.

Once we pay each other to act responsibly toward future generations, it is not a matter of where the process begins, but rather where it will end. Some would claim we are entitled to compensation for acting responsibly in not desecrating a community's water filter (its wetlands). If that is how the takings clause operates, then are there other acts of human kindness, compassion and responsibility meriting reimbursement from the public treasury? Will the public treasury become a brokerage house for options in trustworthiness?

What if zoning laws prohibit you from constructing a fast-food restaurant in a residential zone? This commercial use would likely bring a higher value than residential use. Is the public treasury exposed for the incremental difference between the commercial value and the residential value? How about the fellow deprived of the multi-million dollar value of his residential property if only it could be used for the next toxic waste site? Do we conclude the amount of compensation due under the Fifth is limited only by the land owner's malevolent ingenuity?

The business of using the public treasury to purchase acts of civic responsibility is a dangerous precedent. Will we now also start compensating each other for random acts of charity? The responsible steward would protect the habitat, the wetland, without any expectation of compensation. Should this steward be deprived of the financial rewards conferred upon the less caring person under Regulatory Takings laws?

The law of Regulatory Takings under the Fifth Amendment started with the following quote from Justice Oliver Wendell Holmes, of the U.S. Supreme Court, in 1922:

> while property may be regulated to a certain extent, if a regulation goes too far it will be recognized as a taking.[134]

Distinguishing what's not quite far enough from what's "too far" has intrigued legal scholars for the better part of this century. Measuring how far is "too far" has become the defining legal challenge in the field of Regulatory Takings. Although specific cases may, at times, defy logic[135] it would appear that the outcome is determined by the "felt necessities of the time." Again, in the words of Oliver Wendell Holmes, Jr.:

> The life of the law has not been logic; it has been experience. The felt necessities of the time, the prevalent moral and political theories, intuition of public policy, avowed or unconscious, even the prejudices which judges share with their fellow-men, have a good deal more to do than the syllogism in determining the rules by which men should be governed. The law embodies the story of a nation's development through many centuries, and it cannot be dealt with as if it contained only the axioms and corollaries of a book of mathematics. In order to know what it is, we must

---

[134] *Pennsylvania Coal Co v Mahon*, 260 U.S. 393 (1922).

[135] *Contrast Keystone Bituminous Coal Ass'n v DeBenedictis*, 480 US 470; 107 S Ct 1232; 94 L Ed2d 472 (1987) with *Pennsylvania Coal Co v Mahon*, 260 US 393; 43 S Ct 158; 67 L Ed 322 (1922).

know what it has been, and what it tends to become.[136]

Let's examine how "felt necessities" are perceived in the courts today. Under the present law, a property owner is entitled to compensation if an environmental regulation prohibits essentially "all economically beneficial use of the land" unless the regulation was permitted under "nuisance principles."[137] So what is a nuisance principle? The word "nuisance" is a French word. It means harm.[138]

This is now where the present meets the future. Whether a land owner is entitled to payment for compliance with environmental laws is now a matter of historic "nuisance" law. Before we can look ahead to future consequences, the U.S. Supreme Court has us searching the past.

Just what is a nuisance? In 1926 the U.S. Supreme Court said: "Nuisance may be the right thing in the wrong place— like a pig in the parlor instead of the barnyard."[139]

A respected legal treatise defines nuisance as follows:

> No better definition of a public nuisance has been suggested than that of an act or omission "which obstructs or causes inconvenience or damage to the public in the exercise of rights common to all Her Majesty's subjects." . . . public nuisance includes interference with public health, public safety, public morals, public peace, public comfort and the public convenience in travel.[140]

---

[136] Holmes, Jr., Oliver Wendell, *The Common Law*, Dover Publications, Inc., first published in 1881.

[137] *Lucas v South Carolina Coastal Council*, 505 US 1003 (1992).

[138] Prosser, "Private Action for Public Nuisance," 52 Penn. Law Rev. 997 (1966).

[139] *Village of Euclid v Ambler Realty Co.*, 272 US 375, 388 (1926).

[140] Prosser & Keeton, Torts, 5th Ed., West Publishing Co.

Principles of nuisance law have prohibited the downhill land owner from flooding neighbors by diverting surface water, from adding flowing water to adjoining properties,[141] from generating traffic problems with an otherwise legitimate business,[142] from emitting excessive noise,[143] from emitting excessive smoke,[144] from keeping bees in an urban setting,[145] from manufacturing intoxicating beverages which, at the time, were deemed "hurtful to society,"[146] or from operating a brickyard even though this was the only productive use of the property.[147] Nuisance has also compelled destruction of cedar trees to prevent a disease from infecting nearby apple orchards.[148]

The concept of harmful activities fluctuates with changing social norms, knowledge and context. The laws of this nation evolve. Oleomargarine[149] and beer[150] were considered contraband years ago,

---

[141] *Pezo v Lester*, 284 Mich 369; 279 NW 864 (1938).

[142] *Long Island Court Homeowners v Methner*, 74 Mich App 383; 254 NW2d 57 (1977).

[143] *Smith v Western*, 380 Mich 256; 158 NW2d 463 (1968).

[144] *Smith v City of Ann Arbor*, 303 Mich 476; 6 NW2d 752 (1943).

[145] *People of Redford v McGregor*, 65 Mich App 747; 238 NW2d 183 (1975).

[146] *Mugler v Kansas*, 123 US 623, 663; 8 S Ct 273; 31 L Ed 205 (1887).

[147] *Hadacheck v Sebastian*, 239 US 394; 36 S Ct 143; 60 L Ed 348 (1915).

[148] *Miller v Schoene*, 276 US 272; 48 S Ct 246; 72 L Ed 568 (1928).

[149] *Powell v Pennsylvania*, 127 US 678; 8 S Ct 992; 32 L Ed 253 (1888). Oleomargarine (imitation butter) was bitterly opposed by butter producers and it was illegal.

[150] *Mugler v Kansas*, 123 US 623 (1887).

while Coca Cola® was lawfully made with cocaine.[151]

Today's nuisance laws should evolve to consider the well-being of our successors. But the courts do not always see it that way. An indifference to limits resides at the heart of this issue. As long as the courts envision unlimited frontiers, it will be difficult for a judge to perceive future harm. The Malthusian message is particularly poignant for the judiciary in Regulatory Takings cases.

Principles of nuisance law are pivotal in determining whether a land owner is entitled to compensation for complying with environmental regulations. Whether nuisance principles will look to future harm depends on whether we are willing to confer legal and moral standing upon the unrepresented next generation.

What gets "took" in takings laws? Is it just the public treasury? Just natural amenities? Or might the bond with our children also get "took"? Might it be our sense of responsibility? Who speaks for civic duty? Who guards her legacy? Takings laws uphold the right to plunder and compromise scarce natural resources. But will responsibility to our nation's future just be left to fend for itself?

While the courts vigilantly guard against Regulatory Takings, they do not recognize "givings." In other words, the public treasury is not reimbursed when it enhances the value of someone's land. Your tax dollars may be used to construct the road to a new sports arena, but don't expect the wealthy land owner to reimburse the taxpayer when the adjoining property surges in value. "Givings" from the public treasury could impart a balance to "takings" laws, but this is not recognized in the law.

Takings laws are not the only place our courts can lodge utopian beliefs in inexhaustible resources. Any number of opportunities exist. For example, as indicated in the next section, the court have even converted a prior cause of environmental degradation into an excuse for future harm!

---

[151] *United States v Housley*, 751 F Supp 1446, 1447 (D Nev, 1990).

28

THE PRIOR CAUSE BECOMES A FUTURE EXCUSE

The great and unlooked for discoveries that have taken place of late years in natural philosophy; the increasing diffusion of general knowledge from the extension of the art of printing; the ardent and unshackled spirit of inquiry that prevails throughout the lettered, and even unlettered world; the new and extraordinary lights that have been thrown on political subjects, which dazzle and astonish the understanding; and particularly that tremendous phenomenon in the political horizon, the French revolution, which, like a blazing comet, seems destined either to inspire with fresh life and vigour, or to scorch up and destroy the shrinking inhabitants of the earth, have all concurred to lead many able men into the opinion that we were touching on a period big with the most important changes, changes that would in some measure be decisive of the future fate of mankind.

— Malthus, 1798, Chapter I

OUR COURTS ARE indifferent to limits in a variety of factual settings. This indifference can be subtle, yet monumentally harmful to our successors. A subtle indifference to limits in the Michigan Court of Appeals recently undermined years of hard fought battles in the Legislature.[152] Here's how it happened.

It should not be this way, but economics can be at odds with the environment. Will this become our manifest destiny?

Mesmerized by business reports and ticker tapes, we lapse into a state

---

[152] *Friends of the Crystal River v Kuras Properties*, 554 NW2d 328 (Mich App, 1996).

of indifference to the world around us. The Great Lakes comprise the world's largest body of fresh water, yet industrial toxins now in the aquatic food chain cause us to limit the number of fish we eat. Atmospheric CO_2 levels will double within the next 70 years, yet we increase emissions at ever alarming rates. Over fifty percent of wetlands in the lower 48 states have yielded to economic interests between 1780 and the 1980s,[153] yet we relentlessly continue an assault on the remainder. Global *per capita* food production is waning.[154] Yet we suburbanize 21,000 acres of America's productive farmland every week.

No one seriously claims this rate of wetland and farmland loss can continue indefinitely. Yet we remain indifferent. Who will future historians blame for this bitter legacy?

Environmental degradation commonly results not so much from malicious vandalism as from well-intentioned profit motives in an unregulated setting.

Economic limits are fixed by scarcity. At an earlier stage in the Industrial Revolution, limits on production were established by the limits of human labor. Scarcity was established by the limits of the labor force. At the time, natural resources, our natural capital, appeared to be in unlimited supply. Accordingly, it was not necessary to account for the loss of natural capital. And we didn't. GNP computations and economic indicators have successfully dodged environmental casualties. No need to count the loss of a bountiful asset in seemingly unlimited supply.

Health standards steadily improved during the industrial revolution. Life spans were lengthened, infant mortality declined, immigration increased and productivity soared. Eventually there was no longer a scarcity of labor.

Scarcity nevertheless continues to limit economic activity. Today it is no longer a scarcity of labor, but rather a scarcity of natural capital. Conventional accounting systems, however, still ignore the loss of

---

[153] T.E. Dahl, *Wetland Losses in the United States 1780's to 1980s*, U.S. Dept. of the Interior, Fish and Wildlife Service, Washington D.C., 21 pp. (1990).

[154] Lester R. Brown and Hal Kane, *Full House*, W.W. Norton & Co., 1994.

natural capital, both public and private. It's as though we persevere in peering over the Alleghenies onto a pastoral world of unlimited resources and vast frontiers. Change is afoot.

State and federal laws now protect us against certain environmental hazards. These laws, such as wetland regulations, are designed to protect the residual frontiers and conservation values. These resources provide natural protection to human life; for example, to maintain clean water, to provide flood control and wildlife habitat. Protection becomes a form of enlightened self-interest as it safeguards natural capital for our successors.

Sometimes there is a measure of leniency under the law. The environmental regulations are often relaxed when there is "no feasible and prudent alternative." This makes good common sense and good law. In other words, if a community's bedrock employer needs a few months to install filters, the environmental regulations can be temporarily suspended. From the perspective of the common good, averting the insolvency of the town by temporarily allowing time for a fix may make good sense. There is just "no feasible and prudent alternative."

This phrase is pivotal to many environmental regulations. It is where the protective rubber meets the hazardous road. Natural resource conservation perilously depends on how we construe the phrase: "no feasible and prudent alternative."

Here's how these words were interpreted by the Michigan Court of Appeals in 1996. A business owner hoped to convert natural capital (in this case, wetlands and a navigable stream — a stretch of the Crystal River) into a golf course. A concerned community, through its nonprofit, charitable voice known as The Friends of the Crystal River, insisted the law did not allow treasured natural resources to be converted into cold cash.

The property owner claimed there was no "feasible and prudent alternative" and therefore the wetlands should become expendable under the law. So just exactly what is meant by the phrase "feasible and prudent alternative"? If the standard of proof is too high, there will be no flexibility in the law. If it is too low, then we will have effectively undermined environmental laws.

The phrase had an extensive history even before Michigan adopted its Wetlands Act in 1979. The U.S. Supreme Court and the Michigan Court of Appeals have previously construed this phrase ("feasible and prudent alternative") under federal highway laws and under the Michigan Environmental Protection Act. The courts said this phrase can only be satisfied if there are *"unusual factors"* of an *"extraordinary magnitude"* and *"unique problems."* That's a tough, yet fair, standard of proof.

But the Michigan Court of Appeals found the standard to be met because the owner's golf course would *"increase its competitiveness in the marketplace."* This now becomes the legal basis upon which protected natural capital is exchanged for cash. There were no particularly *"unusual factors."* Nothing of an *"extraordinary magnitude."* No *"unique problems."* Just a quest to "increase its competitiveness in the marketplace." A hope for more profits. An unquenchable crusade for monetary gain.

There's nothing wrong with profits. But when increased profits become our singular value we betray an indifference to limits. Do we really think natural ecosystems will tolerate abuse as long as we hitch our excuse to a heartfelt yearning for more money? Profits cannot trump all other values. Will we also place a value upon clean water purified by wetlands, our natural filter? Upon the amenities of a natural habitat? A placid river unthreatened by random golf balls? Upon a healthy ecosystem?

A healthy ecosystem promotes a healthy economy. A degraded ecosystem means less economy.

If the courts allow aspirations for *increased private profits* to upstage constitutional and legislative protection of natural resources, then we will have made a mockery of all environmental laws. As a practical matter, virtually every natural resource can be exploited for economic gain. That's why environmental laws were adopted in the first place. Handcuffing environmental protection with the private profiteer's avarice and greed is like securing a day care center with a known child molester.

There is also a dangerous self-canceling component to this interpretation of the law. The Court of Appeals excused one property owner from environmental laws to "increase its competitiveness in the marketplace." But according to Hardin's law, "We can never do merely one thing."[155] We should always ask: "And then what?"

The next competitor in the marketplace will likely rely upon the same principle of law. When this competitor wants to shirk an environmental regulation and compromise natural resources, will it be sufficient to claim it is for the noble cause of increasing competitiveness in the marketplace? That's what the Court of Appeals would have us believe.

When this next competitor raises the level of competition, then the first owner's incremental gain will be eroded. In the hopes of reclaiming competitiveness in the marketplace, the first owner will now express a renewed need to increase competitiveness in the marketplace. Accordingly, this owner will again be armed with a reason to circumvent another environmental law. Every increase in competitiveness of one competitor will justify yet another relaxation of environmental protection for another. Each incremental competitive gain cancels out the prior advance as we rachet further into our natural resources. The Court of Appeals' ruling establishes a spiraling precedent from which our heirs will not escape.

Prior ecological losses were caused by an oversight in the accounting system. We failed to confer value upon natural capital. Profit motives unwittingly had free rein over the environmental during much of our industrial history. But don't we know better today? Can't we visualize the frontier's end? Are limits not yet confronting us?

Under the court's decision, profit motives are no longer just a *cause* of environmental degradation. Rather, profit motives now become the deliberate and planned *excuse* for future exploitation. The cause becomes the excuse!

If a business owner's plan to "increase its competitiveness in the marketplace" will defeat environmental protection at the threshold of a new millennium, then we are in desperate need of a lesson in history. Profit motives, greed and competition have led to casualties to our natural history for centuries. How long will we continue clinging to the illusion of vast frontiers and unlimited resources?

The courts are not alone in ignoring the cumulative effect of our

---

[155] Garrett Hardin, *Living Within Limits*, Oxford University Press, 1993.

actions. We too are sometimes ill-equipped to evaluate the long-term effects of our actions. This is evidenced by our ill-conceived degradation of the nation's spectacular viewsheds.

29

INTERIOR VIEWSCAPES

The superior degree of civil liberty which prevailed in America contributed, without doubt, its share to promote the industry, happiness, and population of these states; but even civil liberty, all powerful as it is, will not create fresh land.
— Malthus, 1798, Chapter XVII

THE INDIFFERENCE TO limits leaves an intrusive mark on our most valued retreats and sacred havens.

Captivating views from the interior of our nation's lakes and streams lead to increasing prices for naturally sculpted waterfront properties. Willows and pines welcome wind textured waters. Aquatic life streaks through shaded shores. Reeds lightly slice advancing waves. Timeless reminders of a rich natural history caress the shore.

So we hire our real estate agents and flock to the waterfront parcel. We strive to capture the precious stillness while we can. While it is still with us. We breathe the sweet mix of dew and cedar. It presents a lasting memory. The contrast of waterfront vegetation with the water's turquoise hue creates a cherished image.

With the hope of capturing and preserving the forested, panoramic scenery as a family legacy, we buy the parcel and prepare house plans. But just how will we memorialize the unique charm compelling this acquisition?

Some are eager to eliminate the biodiverse waterfront heritage in favor of their monocultural lawn. Some even make their presence known with bug zappers which briskly eliminate the mosquito eating critters. Premature lake aging and noisy lawnmowers follow in the path of progress. Fertilizers, herbicides and pesticides temporarily suppress nature's dynamics on the waterfront lawn. But they soon migrate to a more permanent home. In the watershed, the chemicals become an enduring part of the food chain.

No small part of the original charm resulted from the naturally diverse amenities. But now, the interior views from our lakes are obscured by overt, self-referential structures. Scale, color and design become combative with the previously pristine sight. Manicured waterfront lawns impose an urban character.

The owner's need to be seen was not to be concealed by any natural wonder. As our unblemished lakes suffer the indignity of other urbanized areas, may we remain mindful of the difference between the owner's need to see and the need to be seen.

A paddle across our many lakes is now like a frenzied freeway drive amid rows of homes and structures. Any residual hope of communion with nature is now crushed by the latest marvel of perverse scientific progress: the jet-ski, a mosquito tethered to a microphone.

Are we indifferent to the limits of modifying an interior viewscape? Do we believe that by maintaining everyone's right to clear-cut waterfront vegetation, we will never reach the point of compromising the inherent value of nature's bounty?

The natural amenities of our lakes and streams are being surrendered to a short-sighted need to "urbanize" the waterfront. As shoreline greenbelts succumb to the owner's need to be seen, our collective legacy is destroyed. A world of biotic diversity awaiting our imagination is poised on the doorstep of our lakes and streams. Once dismantled, it will not soon be restored.

If we remain indifferent to the limits of visual abuse on interior viewscapes, then we will sacrifice not only a prime natural resource, but we will also diminish ourselves in the process.

Part Five

THE NEXT 200 YEARS

The Next 200 Years

A REFLECTION ON the 200 years since the Malthusian Essay reveals his *Essay on the Principle of Population* was not accurate in all respects, but it was more right than wrong. Admittedly, Malthus may not have fully anticipated human ingenuity and resourcefulness in manipulating food production when confronted with impending shortages. Nor did he envision the vast opening of the North and South American continents and Australia. These territories exposed unanticipated lands and resources for the surplus European population. But, to his credit, Malthus was also guarded in his predictions. He did not precisely define when burgeoning human populations would outstrip available resources for sustenance. He observed a progression and the progression continues. We have successfully pushed back the limits for 200 years, but we are now reaching breathtaking heights on his geometric curve. Can we still stay ahead of the game? And do we really want to? Perhaps we can squeeze ten people into a telephone booth, but do we want to? Is that how we want to live? Is this the legacy by which we care to be remembered? Perhaps it becomes a matter of values. Do we value the serenity of natural havens? Do we value the tranquility of life in an uncongested setting? Do we fear the prospects of hostility and violence if we leave a legacy of scarcity? Will we have the heart to responsibly grapple with the ethical issues proffered by Malthus in 1798?

Even today, some will question the validity of Malthusian predictions. For example, in 1994, Julian Simon stated: "We now have in our hands — in our libraries, really — the technology to feed, clothe, and supply

164

energy to an ever-growing population for the next 7 billion years."[156]
On the anniversary of the encyclical Humanae Vitae, the Catholic
bishops announced: "The world's food resources theoretically could
feed 40 billion people."[157] Let's assume technology could enable us to
provide for more people. When we understand that it can take two
generations before current population policies are reflected in a stable
population, why would we foist the gamble on our successors? Why
would we subject them to the congestion? The scarcity? The prospects
for violence and hostility? The more pressing and anticipated
environmental consequences? Why would we deprive them of the
natural havens already subject to an aggressive assault? Moreover, at
some point, we will reach the Malthusian limit. In the words of Paul R.
Ehrlich and Anne H. Ehrlich:

> Consider how long it would take for the 1994 world
> population of 5.6 billion to increase to a size where there were
> *ten human beings for each square meter* of ice-free land on the
> planet. At the 1994 growth rate, it would take only 18
> doublings to bring the population to that point, and the
> population was then doubling every 43 years. Thus, the
> required doubling would only take 18 x 4.3= 774 years —
> somewhat short of 7 billion. After 1900 years at this growth
> rate, the mass of human population would be equal to the
> mass of the earth; after 6000 years, the mass of the human
> population would equal the mass of the universe.[158]

Are we on the brink of misery and vice? (The nightly news assuredly
leaves this impression.) Some have read the Malthusian *Essay on the*

---

[156] N. Meyers and Julian Simon, *Scarcity or Abundance: A Debate on the Environment*,
W.W. Norton, 1994, p. 65.

[157] Washington Post, Nov. 1988, p. C-15.

[158] Paul R. Ehrlich and Anne H. Erhlich, *Betrayal of Science and Reason*, Island Press,
1996, p. 66.

Principle of Population as a bitter forecast of doom and gloom. Some will glean only pessimism from this bicentennial Malthusian essay.

On the other hand, others will sense a glimmer of optimism from Malthusian passages. We actually might find comfort on our next frontier. Unlike the outward bound conquests of the past, the next frontier lies closer to home. It will involve a realistic assessment of where we are, and how we got here. Barriers to this next frontier result from our inhibitions. From our unwillingness to see ourselves as an integral part of an ecosystem. From our reluctance to concede we're a fragile and tenuous component of nature's biodiverse web of life.

The next frontier resides within us. In our hearts and minds. We are no longer poised on the frontier of our forebears. The frontier out there. Today, the frontier is in here. It is a matter of introspection.

How we fare during the next 200 years, until the Malthusian quadricentennial, may depend on how we scale the barriers of this frontier. Here are a few considerations:

1. Numeracy. It is difficult to assess our impact to the surrounding ecosystem if progress is gauged only by our biological clocks. Day-to-day changes are insignificant. Alterations from one season to the next are not noticed. Annual changes can be particularly imperceptible.

Only by averaging several decades or centuries can we meaningfully evaluate the cumulative impact of throughput and resource depletion.

Numeracy is the mathematical equivalent of literacy. Can we escape the concealed geometric sequences of pro-growth advocates? Can we responsibly assess our place on the charts? It is a matter of doubling times: 2, 4, 8, 16, 32, 64, 128, 256, 512, 1024, 2048, 4096, etc. The charts on population, CO_2, fossil fuel depletion, solid waste streams, or world fish stock depletion charts all look much the same. They present a geometric progression.

Visions of vast frontiers become an illusion in a numerate light. The effect of surging numbers brings the frontier to our doorstep in a heartbeat.

Numeracy also involves an appreciation of delayed response times. America's decision to begin reducing fertility on about the time of Earth Day 1970 will not be reflected in a population plateau until approximately 60 to 70 years later.[159]

Policies and practices implemented today may not come to fruition in our lifetime. The planter of an olive tree knows it may take 60 years for the tree to mature and bear fruit. The planter would seldom live long enough to partake in the fruits of this labor. That was not a deterrent to planting the seeds for others within the planter's radius of altruism. The olive planter selflessly chose to benefit others. People he may never meet.

Similar choices confront us today. Successorship on the planet remains an inter-generational relay race. The baton we transfer to our followers merits cautious and numerate care.

2. Values. What's important to us?

Can we find fulfillment in our obedient response to mass merchandisers? If we are to begin striking a balance between ourselves and the ecosystem, between the present and the future, then arresting our frenzied state of consumption would be a good start.

This is not a pitch for austerity. It is a plea for balance and values. It will require cutting back on excessive consumption and multiplication. Immediate self-gratification isn't all it's cracked up to be anyway. Our subservient response to the glitz of mass merchandisers impoverishes our sense of independence. How can we be free if we are mere pawns on someone's economic chessboard? The belief that we exercise independent choices, that over-consumption is the product of our free will, is an illusion. It borders on delusional.

If our values are set by the wild imagery of Fifth Avenue profiteers, then our pervasive sense of emptiness should come as no surprise. Our endless quest for self-identity, freedom and liberty will remain unfulfilled. As mindless soldiers on someone else's economic battlefield, it is time to stage an uprising. To conquer the next frontier. To break the tyrannical bonds of destructive consumption. To re-acquaint ourselves with ourselves.

As we float like flotsam and jetsam amid a shopping culture, might it be helpful to take a minute for introspection? What features do we

---

[159] Roy Beck, *Re-Charting America's Future,* The Social Contract Press, 1994.

identify as character?

Is self-esteem now measured by our propensity to shop for the sake of shopping? To shop till we drop? To consume for the sake of consumption? To discard for the sake of a fashion industry? Can we really purchase self-esteem at the mega-mall? Perhaps we may still heed the classic New England maxim: "Use it up, wear it out; Make it do, or do without."[160]

Or is self-esteem a measure of a more internal quality? Could it have something more to do with our willingness to consider others? To harbor thoughtfulness in a safe dwelling place? To express compassion for our successors in daily choices and in stewardship of the land?

Might self-esteem and character also have something to do with traditional pillars of character, such as trustworthiness, respect, responsibility, fairness, caring and citizenship?[161] How do personal accomplishments fit into the hierarchy of values today?

3. **Ethical Compromises.** Our children stand to inherit a devalued future. Are we simply uncaring? Is there a scarcity of parental care?

There is usually no shortage of good motives. Degraded surroundings can result from the cumulative effect of well-intentioned, but misguided, decisions.

For example, the board of directors and officers of a modern corporation which confronts environmental harm in its daily business have a singular duty in the eyes of the law. They owe a so-called "fiduciary duty" to the corporation. This legal obligation can be construed as requiring them to maximize profits for the shareholders. The shareholders own the corporation. As owners, they derive the profits generated by the workers, the officers and the board of directors.

The officers and board of this corporation, which regularly rivals the

---

[160] John Bartlett, *Bartlett's Familiar Quotations*, Little, Brown and Co, Fifteenth Edition, 1980, p. 924.

[161] Michael Josephson, *Making Ethical Decisions*, Josephson Institute of Ethics, 3d Ed.; James Q. Wilson, *The Moral Sense*, The Free Press, 1993.

ecology, must discharge their duty within the bounds of the law. The officers and board members may not consider it within their province to make financial sacrifices in favor of the environment. Their legal (and fiduciary) duty can in some instances be considered strictly economic. The courts often compel the board to exercise their discretion under the "*business* judgment rule." This might not necessarily coincide with sound environmental judgment. Environmental and economic considerations can coincide, but when they do not, profit motives can prevail in the decision-making process by people believing themselves to be constrained by the "bottom line."

The environmental decisions of a corporation can thus come to rest upon the shoulders of the officers and the board of directors. The fiduciary responsibilities, however, might compel them to do no than more than is absolutely essential to bring the corporation into compliance with the law. Salinating rivers with gas-drilling operations can become a fiduciary duty if it is permitted by the law. The clear-cut of old growth timber might be compelled unless strictly prohibited. A competitive marketplace will not lament the loss of a corporation striving to uphold the integrity of the ecosystem at the expense of corporate profitability. The marketplace is unforgiving.

The tough choices between environmental degradation and profits are often illusory in the corporations deriving profits by imposing on the natural surroundings. If the officers and board believe their legal duty is to maximize profits, then "future abuse" is likely to follow. Mother Nature will not always win at this game.

The shareholders of these corporations derive the profits and count their earnings in a remote and comfortable setting. The stock broker's office is not adorned with artwork celebrating a clear-cut. Financial decisions are made in an antiseptic setting. Participants are distanced from the dirty work and they are not necessarily caused to be fettered by environmental casualties. They may not be caused to grapple with the tough choices. The tough decisions could have been made by the board governed by a set of "ethical" principles and fiduciary duties which might require them to maximize profits for the shareholders. This system can operate to discourage the officers and board from considering environmental consequences. It can enable the shareholders to sweep in on white horses to collect the profits at a comfortable distance with a clean conscience. Ticker tapes are monitored tapes at a safe distance. Shareholders read their stock reports at a remote location from the stench of toxic landfills and from the dispiriting remains of a clear-cut or strip mine.

Where the corporation is directly engaged in profiting from environmental casualties, it's as though the corporate structure and legal system was designed to immunize the shareholders from meaningful ethical considerations for our surroundings. The environment is just not part of the deliberative process in this corporate legal structure.

This is not intended to condemn all corporate employees and there surely are responsible persons operating in corporate settings. Nevertheless, as we attempt to identify a possible plan for launching into the next 200 years, we might make the observation that it can be difficult to find a legal obligation for future generations in the polluting corporation's legal setting.

Accordingly, the tough choices might not be made. The shareholders can be liberated from many environmental decision-making responsibilities, and the board of directors could feel constrained by a strict duty to maximize profits. Under the existing corporate system, the players may discharge their responsibilities honorably, the fiduciary duties can be met, and profits can be turned. Yet all the well-intentioned actors sometimes can become co-conspirators in a sinister plot to dishonor the future.

As a first step toward reclaiming a sense of responsibility, the system should, by law, transfer the tough choices to the shareholders who, after all, derive the profits. When actions of the corporation entail a risk of endangering natural ecosystems, the decision should be made by someone other than the officers or board operating under the fiduciary duty to maximize profits.

Why not require the beneficiaries of the ultimate profits to decide? Whenever the decision involves a risk to the environment, why not remove the decision from the board? Why not compel the shareholders to decide whether their incremental profits are worth more than the incremental loss to the ecosystem? Under this system, our successors would at least be protected by the prospect for a conscience to emerge.

This might impart a reasoned thought process. The shareholders could, under this system, also derive the satisfaction of knowing their attendance at corporate meetings can serve a higher goal than may be derived from sheer profit motives. The existing system, in contrast, deliberately turns a deaf ear to conservation.[162]

4. **Associations.** John Muir reminds us "When we try to pick out anything by itself, we find it hitched to everything else in the universe."[163]

Hardin's law tells us: "We can never do merely one thing."[164] Dr. Hardin recommends we ask: "And then what?" It is an elemental rule of physics that every action prompts a reaction. He explains this in human terms as follows:

Wishing to kill insects, we may put an end to the singing of the birds. Wishing to "get there" faster, we insult our lungs with smog. Wishing to know what is happening everywhere in the world at once, we create an information overload against which the mind rebels, responding by a new and dangerous apathy.[165]

A connective tissue binds us to the Earth's natural systems and to each other. We tend to view our actions in isolation. But there is a connectivity to life.

We are quick to identify the cause of the *Exxon Valdez* oil spill. The captain was intoxicated and tanker ran aground. By popular consensus, alcohol and an over-indulgent tanker captain are a dangerous mix on

---

[162] Andrew Bard Schmoolker, *The Illusion of Choice*, State University of New York Press, 1993.

[163] John Muir, *My First Summer in the Sierra*, Penguin Nature Library, 1987 (first published in 1911).

[164] Garrett Hardin, *Living Within Limits*, Oxford University Press, 1993, p. 199.

[165] Garrett Hardin, "The Cybernetics of Competition," *Perspectives in Biology and Medicine*, 7 (1963): 58-84.

the high seas. And that became the cause. First the captain was drunk. Then the ship ran aground. Grounding followed intoxication therefore intoxication caused grounding. Is this sound logic?

Our gluttonous appetite for cheap fossil fuels wasn't even considered as a contributing factor. And while we decry the effects of the oil spill on the ecosystem, we weren't exactly planning to be good stewards with the fossil fuel in any event. Instead of conspicuously spilling it into Prince William Sound, our disposal plans were less poignant. We planned to burn it and then dump it in the atmospheric sink. But that's no cause to dampen our hostility toward the glassy eyed tanker captain. The outrage warranted a venting opportunity, and he was readily accessible.

Is it too late on the ecological clock to shirk accountability? Hopefully not. But there's nevertheless still time to strike meaningful associations. There's still time to stop pointing an outward bound finger. And there's room to share responsibility.

It's not just a matter of shopping for another unnecessary article. We're hooked into a bigger system. There's a layer of connectivity between our actions and the surroundings. This purchase and that strip mine are connected. So is this car and that smog. And this waste and that landfill.

Wherever we turn, we find relationships in an interconnected world.

By rendering ourselves dependant on the motor vehicle, we unnecessarily deplete scarce reserves of fossil fuel, add unwanted CO_2 to the greenhouse effect, and require highway engineers to plan more pavement in our lives. More highways compel more glow-in-the-dark parking lagoons to surround featureless, architecturally uneventful, bunker-like mass merchandising boxes that impoverish our sense of community. This diminishes the sense of civic duty otherwise present in a quaint small town setting. Associations abound.

And by lining up at the checkout counter to purchase unneeded merchandise, we are casting a ballot in favor of the promoters of excessive consumption. This ballot subsidizes the advertiser's effort to claim yet another part of our soul. And our independent sense of freedom is thus further distracted by their dazzling imagery. We become further corrupted into believing that our existing possessions are functionally or aesthetically obsolete. Even more unnecessary merchandise is then foisted upon us. The waste stream increases. The depletion of resources escalates. And we are further deluded into thinking we're somehow "better off."

The air exhaled by Thomas Robert Malthus nourished a tree now 200 years old. His exhaled CO_2 was converted to molecular oxygen in a photosynthetic process. The oxygen cycled throughout the plant and animal kingdom. At times it may have been trapped beneath surging waters, bringing life to an aquatic ecosystem. It cooled the brow of the colonists and the Native American. It cycled through a mother's soft breath upon her infant child. The same air molecules encountered the impurities we more recently discarded in the atmospheric sink. Now tainted, the molecules continue to cycle through life's processes. What's the likelihood we have, at some time in our life, inhaled the same Malthusian molecule? Imponderables breed associations.

It is a matter of associations. Recognizing connections. Relating current actions to future harms. Understanding we cannot do merely one thing. Appreciating our place in the scheme of things. Placing a value on the natural systems upon which our lives depend and learning how virtually every choice we make is inescapably associated with this system.

If we refuse to make the associations, if we decline this educational opportunity, if we arrogantly believe we're above the system, if we lack the humility to make these connections, then we'll suffer yet another indignity beyond the environmental casualties. Once lost it will be difficult to reclaim. And if it is beyond reclamation, then even our humanity and civility hang perilously in the balance.

To endanger the art of drawing associations is to ultimately imperil even our ability to strike meaningful associations with each other.

EPILOGUE

A WALK IN the woods might be one of our most highly under-rated activities.

A two-mile thick glacier blanketed much of Michigan about 14,000 years ago. As the glacier retreated it unveiled a densely compressed land mass adjoining the body of water geologists now call Lake Algonquin. Remnants of Lake Algonquin eventually formed much of the Great Lakes.[166] The glacially compressed land rebounded in northwestern Michigan in two stages. The first rebound of about 10,000 years ago raised Lake Algonquin's shoreline above the water level.

Algonquin's eroded, and now exposed, shore lies at the end of our street. This stretch of the elevated coast has become a protected nature preserve.[167] Walking trails are maintained. Naturalists and conservationists are welcomed.

---

[166] John A. Dorr, Jr and Donald F. Eschman, *Geology of Michigan,* The University of Michigan Press, 1970, p. 177. W. R. Farrand, *The Glacial Lakes Around Michigan,* Geological Survey Division, Michigan Department of Natural Resources, Bulletin 4, Revised 1988.

[167] The nature preserve is maintained by the Bay View Association, a residential community on the edge of Petoskey, Michigan. Land conservation efforts are also implemented by the Little Traverse Conservancy, the Walloon Conservancy, Tip of the Mitt Watershed Council, Sierra Club's Mackinaw Chapter-Algonquin Group, Michigan Dept. of Natural Resources, and a variety of other non-profit organizations in this region.

Our yellow lab Kassie and I descend the abandoned Algonquin shore into the preserve's cathedral country. Here the welcoming hardwood air makes us feel like privileged intruders in a primeval landscape. Here the seasons throb with the fullness of life. Here the early morning sun gilds the peaks of towering trees. Here the light and shadows dance with the wind-tossed understory during the day. Here the tree limbs become silhouetted against the night sky. Here myriad forms of life find ingenious ways to secure and disperse their seeds. Here the cost of a beetle's refrain from venturing out for food is starvation. Here the price of its quest can become a mercifully swift death as it becomes food for others in a timeless cycle. Here a mating, cunning and propagating world of discovery awaits our patient inquiry.

This is where the trees' mossy limbs stroke textured waters. Here the summer rain brings intensity to the landscape. Lightning shatters time. Here we can swat enough mosquitoes and black flies to ponder our rightful place in the food chain. Here the attentive broadwinged hawk clings to the sky on its wings and chickadees flutter through heavy humus-scented air. Here ferns commemorate the first terrestrial settlers on a moss-carpeted river bank.

This rare biodiverse land thrives alongside the human enterprise. Here's a safe place to perceive the pain for similar places objectified for economic gain. This place becomes a fragile refuge amid rapidly vanishing surroundings.

The entertainment industry and modern media cause us to develop a stubborn demand for swift information. Wildlife can become motionless and pallid in nature's deafening silence unless we learn to subdue this demand. Here patience reigns supreme. We can resonate with nature's cadence, but only by shedding expectations of swift entertainment nurtured by the TV industry.

This is the land on which our son's eager eyes first became inquisitive while riding on dad's shoulders. It's a blurred image of startled deer in our path. It's the fictitious squirrel's bridge overhead. It's met with the hope that someday he'll reflect on the time spent on dad's shoulders while trekking the same path, perhaps carrying the next generation into the future. And if he can experience it, so can many others. Perhaps in the heat of summer. Maybe in the steamy morning mist.

In the scope of modern human experience, can we still perceive the soft decomposing humus underfoot in one of nature's great transformations? Can we still appreciate the insect's mating ritual in the vibrant air? Can we still value the drama of the queen ant shedding her wings after her once-in-a-lifetime-mid-air sexual encounter. Can we still grieve the fate of her suitors, each of which will surrender his life for this singular experience?

For Kassie, a keen sense of smell is commonly dulled by detergents, bleaches, cleaners, dust and non-biodegradable fabrics around the house. She enthusiastically responds to the word "walk," and even the letters "w-a-l-k." For her, it marks the prospect of another venture into the preserve. It's a matter of fresh air, running, bounding, splashing and most of all, inhaling the scents. Her imagery acquired from the passing fragrance runs wild. The residual essence of a scampering squirrel, rabbit, a mating message or a territorial warning are broadcast by wind borne scents. Our less-developed senses leave us with a sharply curtailed imagination. The mental images prompted by her busy nose might be the canine equivalent of a human's outing to an art museum.

Forested thoughts mask the reality of "progress" just beyond the preserve's edge. We pierce but a thin veneer of civilization. Trudging the bottomlands of what was Lake Algonquin several millennia ago becomes only a temporary escape. A momentary opportunity to make associations. To experience the connectivity of life. To humbly acknowledge our place in the scheme of things.

The expression of gratitude for this rich experience is afflicted with the prospect of vanishing forests. Natural havens are threatened not so much by maliciousness or vandalism, but rather by an indifference to limits.

Eventually we ascend the former lake bed of Algonquin's eroded shore. Kassie's tail no longer wags with the same enthusiasm. Upon leaving the forested realm, the textured mosaic of life, the rich setting, we again enter the world of pavement and genetically-engineered lawns. Here the green grass is doused with life-threatening chemicals to suppress all but the selected hybrid lawn.

The forest's ingenious mosaic of life, on the other hand, represents nature's intellect. Each fiber of life adds wisdom to the mind of the forest. There's a logically coherent pattern, and a clarity of thought, even in nature's seemingly chaotic patterns. As threads in life's rich web are eliminated on our monocultural lawns and recreational areas, the land's IQ plummets. We might see the clear-cut as proof of human superiority, but we leave the land in a stupider condition. It's dumbed-down to suit our short-sighted convenience.

Most species roaming our created habitat are not likely to survive the harsh herbicides and pesticides. But if they do, they'll be handed a fatal blow by their arch rival: the weed puller and its owner. In all his polyester glory, he'll hoist the severed weed by the puller for the world to behold. It's as if he's heralding the conquest of a dreaded foe to once again claim the heart of his fair maiden. Chivalry hasn't died. It has just taken on a new face. It is still a matter of conquest. Instead of a lance, we now substitute the weed puller. And instead of armor, we now prefer the more breathable polyester.

There's no room for dreams to run free on this lawn. This is singular. It's monocultural. A modern day clear-cut. Gone is a biodiverse heritage. Extirpated are the migrant species. Forgotten are the pollinators. Sequestered are the critters. Estranged is our natural history. And endangered is our imaginative potential.

We live in a county of 27,000 people. This is one of 83 counties in Michigan. The latest draft of our county's master land-use plan calls for a "build-out" of almost one million people! Michigan has been a nine-million person state for several decades. In other words, the local master plan is designed around the principle that one out of every nine

Michigan residents will someday land in this county. Maintaining an agricultural legacy, forested retreats and open space will be a challenge under this plan. Between now and the time that one in nine Michigan residents actually arrive, urbanization will continue to be a sporadic, haphazard, fragmenting and chaotic experience. Our unfortunate experience is being shared under countless other master plans across the land.

The master plan isn't a deliberately diabolical plan. It has been assembled by well-intentioned, caring folk. Much of the effort was generously contributed by concerned community members. But even the well-intentioned can harbor an indifference to limits. Unless land itself can be seen as a scarce resource, unless we can break the romantic mystique of the frontier, unless we concede that haphazard fragmentation of the land is a one-way ratchet (we only rachet in, not out) and unless we respect the finite natural amenities, it will be difficult to impart a land ethic in land-use plans.

Kassie awakens us at night as she sleeps on the family bed. She recalls the forested experience with vivid detail. The aroma of detergent on our bed quilt is no deterrent. She visualizes the passing stumps, crevices and grasses as the scented vegetation wafts by. Her senses are again aroused by the sights and sounds. Her spirit rushes forward as her heart responds to the pace. She darts toward images as she bounds forward in her sleep. She envisions a scampering squirrel and hastens in pursuit. She mentally retraces her earlier footsteps with twitches and reflexive bolts. But alas, she will again suffer humiliation at the hands of the scolding squirrel, now safely perched on a tree. She utters a muffled bark and springs to the tree in her fantasy, but without avail. Another muffled bark. Even in her dreams the prey once again eludes her pursuit. Rewarded by the chase, she again slips into a vacuous slumber. And so do we.

Our teen-age son remains captivated by the lure of commercial TV. His dad, a sentimental country lawyer, is no match for the stratagems of well-funded media tycoons. The quest for nature's well-kept secrets, for information on nature's terms, and at her pace, is pale by comparison to the dazzling lure of TV. His appreciation of the world around him is gradually awakening, but it will still take time for him to understand that the status of the endangered piping plover in the wild is a measure of his health. It's his eventual legacy. There resides his security in life's mosaic.

How may we preserve natural history for our successors? This becomes our defining challenge. How can we make this place safe for them? How can we cling to the wildness? How may we preserve the beauty, the hope, the serenity, the mystery for them?

Every time he calls for his father, it prompts a promise again. Every time. It's a promise to safeguard nature's legacy. Not just for him, but for his friends, his peers, and our successors. For the natural amenities. For the natural history. For a land ethic. For conservation. And even if it's only to preserve, for them, a margin of safety and the privilege of wonder.

BIBLIOGRAPHY

Abernethy, Virginia D. Ph.D. *Population Politics*, New York: Insight Books, 1993.

Beck, Roy. *Re-Charting America's Future*, The Social Contract Press, Petoskey, Michigan, 1994.

Beck, Roy. *The Case Against Immigration*, New York: W.W. Norton & Co., 1996.

Bouvier, Leon F. and Lindsey Grant. *How Many Americans?*, San Francisco: Sierra Club Books,   1994.

Brimelow, Peter. *Alien Nation*, New York: Random House, 1995.

Brown, Lester R. and Hal Kane. *Full House*, New York: W.W. Norton & Co., 1994.

Brown, Lester R. *Who Will Feed China?*, New York: W.W. Norton & Co., 1995.

Daly, Herman E. *Beyond Growth*, Boston: Beacon Press, 1996.

de Waal, Frans. *Good Natured*, Cambridge, Massachusetts: Harvard University Press, 1996.

Ehrlich, Paul R. and Anne H. Ehrlich. *Betrayal of Science and Reason*, Washington, D.C.: Island Press, 1996.

Geyer, Georgie Anne. *Americans No More*, New York: The Atlantic Monthly Press, 1996.

Gore, Al. *Earth in the Balance*, Boston: Houghton Mifflin Co., 1992.

Gould, Stephen Jay. *Full House*, New York: Harmony Books, 1996.

Graham, Jr., Otis L. *A Limited Bounty*, New York: The McGraw-Hill Companies, Inc., 1996.

Hardin, Garrett. *Living Within Limits*, New York: Oxford University Press,

1993.

Hardin, Garrett. *The Immigration Dilemma: Avoiding the Tragedy of the Commons*, Washington, D.C.: Federation for American Immigration Reform, 1995.

Hylton, Thomas. *Save our Land, Save our Towns*, Harrisburg, Pennsylvania: R.B. Books, 1995.

Katz, Peter. *The New Urbanism*, New York: McGraw-Hill, Inc., 1994.

Kennedy, Paul. *Preparing for the 21ˢᵗ Century*, New York: Random House, 1993.

Kunstler, James Howard. *Geography of Nowhere*, New York: Simon & Shuster, 1993.

Kunstler, James Howard. *Home From Nowhere*, New York: Simon & Shuster, 1996.

Lutton, Wayne and John Tanton. *The Immigration Invasion*, Petoskey, Michigan: The Social Contract Press, 1994.

Malthus, Thomas Robert. *An Essay on the Principle of Population*, New York: Oxford University Press (reprint of original 1798 publication), 1993.

Noss, Reed F. and Allen Y. Cooperrider. *Saving Nature's Legacy*, Washington, D.C.: Island Press, 1994.

Sandel, Michael J. *Democracy's Discontent*, Cambridge, Massachusetts: Belknap Press of Harvard University Press, 1996.

Tanton, John H. M.D. "End of the Migration Epoch," Petoskey, Michigan: *The Social Contract*, Vol. IV, No. 3, Spring, 1994.

Wilson, Edward O. *The Diversity of Life*, Cambridge, Massachusetts: Belknap Press of Harvard University Press, 1992.

Wright, Robert. *The Moral Animal*, New York: Vintage Books, 1994.

APPENDIX

The following nonprofit organizations are actively involved in one or more of the issues addressed in this bicentennial essay. Surely there are others to whom apologies are respectfully offered for the innocent oversight.

Major National Groups with U.S. Focus

Carrying Capacity Network
2000 P St., NW, Ste. 240
Washington, DC 20036
202/296-4548, fax: 202/296-4609
email: ccn@igc.apc.org

Federation for American Immigration Reform
1666 Connecticut Ave, NW, Ste 400
Washington, DC 20077
202/328-7004
http://www.fairus.org

Negative Population Growth NPG
210 The Plaza
P.O. Box 1206
Teaneck, NJ 07666
201/837-3555 fax: 202/837-0288

Donald Mann, President
Washington office:
1666 Connecticut Ave, Ste 400
Washington, DC 20077
202/667-8950 fax: 202/387-3447
Sharon McCloe-Stein, Executive Director

Population-Environment Balance
2000 P St., NW, Ste 210
Washington, DC 20036
202/955-5700 fax: 202/955-6161

Zero Population Growth
1400 16th St., NW, Ste 320
Washington, DC 20036
202/332-2200 / 800/767-1956
fax: 202/332-2302
e-mail: zpg@igc.apc.org
http://www.zpg.org

Major National Groups with Population Programs

Izaak Walton League,
Carrying Capacity Project
707 Conservation Lane
Gaithersburg, MD 20878-2983
301/548-0150 fax: 301/548-0149
Ben Hren, Project Director

League of Women Voters
Population Coalition
226 West Foothills Blvd., Ste C
Claremont, CA 91711
909/625-5717
http://home.earthlink.net/mhempel/popco
Marilyn Hempel, director

National Audubon Society
Human Population and Resource Use Dept.
Patricia Waak, Director
4150 Darley Ave, Ste 7
Boulder, CO 80303
303/499-5155 fax: 303/499-0223

NAS Population Program
666 Pennsylvania Ave, SE
Washington, DC 20003
202/547-9009

National Wildlife Federation
Population Program
1400 16th St., NW
Washington, DC 20036
202/939-3311 fax: 202/797-6646

Major National Groups with Population Concerns

Sierra Club
Population Program, Local Carrying Capacity Campaign
408 C St., NE
Washington, DC 20002
202/547-ll41

Union of Concerned Scientists
26 Church St.
Cambridge, MA 02238

National Resources Defense Council
1200 New York Ave, NW, Ste 400
Washington, DC 20005
202/289-6868
Population Program: Jacqueline Hamilton

Wilderness Society
900 17th St., NW
Washington, DC 20006
202/833-2300 fax: 202/429-3958
Counselor Gaylord Nelson

Other Population Groups with U.S. Focus

National Optimum Trust Effort
1070 SE Denman Avenue
Corvallis, OR 97333
503/752-4383
M. Boyd Wilcox, Founder

Population Communication
1250 E. Walnut St., Ste 220
Pasadena, CA 91106
818/793-4750 fax: 818/793-4791
email: popcommla@aol.com

Population Education Committee
11646 W. Pico Blvd, Ste 23
Los Angeles, CA 90064
310/268-2828 fax: 310/268-2832

Other Population Groups

The Social Contract
316-1/2 East Mitchell St.
Petoskey, MI 49770
616/347-1171 fax: 616/347-1185
email: soccon@freeway.net

Alan Guttmacher Institute
120 Wall Street
New York, NY 10005
212/248-1111 fax:212/248-l951

Poptech
Population Technical Assistance Project
1611 North Kent St., Ste 508
Arlington, VA 22209
703/247-8630 fax: 703/247-8640
email: poptech@bhm.com
Established by USAID in 1970 to assist in conducting population sector assessments, program or project evaluations.

Population Reference Bureau
1875 Connecticut Ave, NW, Ste 520
Washington DC 20009
202/483-1100 fax: 202/328-3937
email: popref@prb.org
http://www.prb.org/prb/

The Population Institute
107 Second Street, NE
Washington, DC 20002
202/544-3300

INDEX

Additional Information

If copies of *A Bicentennial Malthusian Essay* are not readily available at your local bookstore, you may order copies by calling the publisher, Rhodes & Easton, at:

(800)706-4636

For comments you may wish to offer the author, you may write the author, via the publisher, at:

Rhodes & Easton
121 East Front Street, 4th Floor
Traverse City, Michigan 49684

Alternatively, you may e-mail the author at:

rohe@freeway.net

Or, visit the Malthus website for further information:

www.trmalthus.com